THE BEST OF SAINSBURY'S

VEGETARIAN COOKING

THE BEST OF SAINSBURY'S

VEGETARIAN COOKING

CONTENTS

CONTRIBUTORS

Main author: Caroline Ellwood

Contributing authors: Michelle Berriedale Johnson, Carol Bowen, Gill Edden, Claire Ferguson, Wendy Godfrey, Naomi Good, Carole Handslip, Norma MacMillan, Rhona Newman, Julia Roles

Special Photography: David Gill

NOTES

Standard spoon measures are used in all recipes
1 tablespoon = one 15 ml spoon
1 teaspoon = one 5 ml spoon
All spoon measures are level.

Size 3 eggs should be used unless otherwise stated.

Ovens should be preheated to the specified temperature.

For all the recipes, quantities are given in both metric and imperial measures. Follow either set but not a mixture of both because they are not interchangeable.

If fresh yeast is unobtainable, substitute dried yeast but use only half the recommended quantity and follow the manufacturer's instructions for reconstituting.

Fresh herbs are used unless otherwise stated. If unobtainable substitute a bouquet garni of the equivalent dried herbs or use dried herbs instead but halve the quantities stated.

Published exclusively for
J Sainsbury plc
Stamford House
Stamford Street,
London SE1 9LL
by Reed International Books Limited
Michelin House
81 Fulham Road
London SW3 6RB

First published in Great Britain in 1992

ISBN 0 600 57694 9

Produced by Mandarin Offset
Printed and Bound in Hong Kong

INTRODUCTION

Here at last is a really practical guide to healthy and creative eating without meat, fish or poultry for you, your family and friends to enjoy. It's packed with wonderful recipes for vegetarians that aren't cranky, complicated or laborious – just simply nutritious recipes using the best of foods in season and some wholefoods. That is not to say that the pleasures of life like chocolate, meringue and cream have been forgotten – vegetarian food still has its full complement of indulgent treats!

Although written principally for people who want to eat well without eating meat, the following pages also have something to offer meat-eating diners too. There are sustaining soups for starters; bright ideas for beginnings to meals, formal or informal; mouth-watering main meal suggestions using pasta, rice, cheese, pulses, tofu, grains and a whole host of vegetables; many promising puddings to round off a meal; a fresh batch of baked breads, cakes and pastries for the sweet and savoury toothed; and many mouth-watering recipes for vegetable, salad or meal accompaniments.

Many of the recipes are foreign in origin – hardly surprising when the majority of people in this world are vegetarian (it is only in the affluent West that meat is served daily). So you will be able to feast on Indian curries, Chinese stir-fry dishes as well as layered pasta Italian specialities to name just a few.

Feeling healthier and socially more responsible may be just two of the benefits you will enjoy with vegetarian eating but undoubtedly you will also appreciate the greater spending power you'll have by buying such foods. Meat, fish and poultry are expensive so you'll be eating in a more economical way by introducing vegetarian dishes to your meal table, even if it isn't every day of the week.

WHY VEGETARIAN?

Vegetarianism is certainly a healthier way of eating. Many of our Western diseases are of recent origin and diet-related. Too great an intake of animal fats, salt and sugar leads to a dramatic increase in the incidence of heart disease, diabetes and obesity, while other diseases, such as diverticulitis and cancer of the bowel, are directly related to lack of fibre in the diet.

An increase in the general consumption of fresh vegetables and foods rich in plant protein at the expense of animal protein helps vegetarians to prevent what we have come to call 'civilized diseases'.

ALTERNATIVE FOODS
Meat, poultry and fish are prime sources of the protein essential to health, so the vegetarian must seek alternative sources. These can be found in nuts, seeds, legumes (beans and pulses) and,to a lesser extent, in whole grains. These sources also contain fibre, which plays an essential part in the way the body handles the food we eat, but they do not contain the saturated animal fats which are harmful to health. Whilst individual ingredients may sometimes appear expensive, it can be cheaper to eat nuts, fruit and vegetables than meat!

When adopting this new way of eating, you must ensure that you achieve a properly balanced diet. There are four main food groups within a vegetarian diet: beans, nuts and seeds; grains; dairy produce; and fruit and vegetables. If you include something from each group in your daily diet you will be sure of getting all the nutrients you need.

PLANNING MEALS
Embarking on a new style of eating will inevitably mean more time spent in the planning and preparation of meals at first. It is in fact no more difficult to cook vegetarian food than any other, but it will take a little time to become accustomed to new methods and to know which foods are best served together.

Try to include a different grain, bean or pulse dish whenever possible so that you discover different combinations of flavours and textures. In particular, it is important to remember that you are no longer tied to the traditional 'meat and 2 veg' concept. Vegetarian cookery is a rich and varied cuisine, full of many marvellous dishes with definite characteristics. It encompasses many foreign specialities and may comprise of several equally important courses or several dishes served at once. The following guidelines are useful:

- Use wholemeal flour and pasta and brown rice – all of which have more flavour than their white equivalents.
- Breadcrumbs, preferably wholemeal, are used in many recipes and it is a good idea to keep a supply in the freezer for use at a moment's notice.
- Beans are used extensively, so cook large quantities, bag them in usable portions and freeze; they'll then be ready for use within an hour.
- Always keep the water in which you have boiled vegetables for use as a stock. For extra flavour use shoyu (see page 7), yeast extract or vegetable concentrates.

SPECIALIST INGREDIENTS

Nuts and Seeds
Nuts and seeds are a high protein food, rich in B vitamins and minerals. Their high fat content is rich in linoleic acid.

Oils and Fats
Oils are one of the essentials of our diet, containing lecithin, vitamins A, E and K, and minerals. Fats and oils can be divided into three kinds: saturated, mono-unsaturated and polyunsaturated. Animal fats, which are solid at room temperature, are high in saturated fats. Excessive consumption of these fats is associated with heart disease. Most vegetable oils are high in polyunsaturated oils. These are preferable because they are thought to lower the level of cholesterol in the blood. Polyunsaturated oils include safflower, sunflower, sesame and corn oil. Olive oil is mono-unsaturated and can be regarded as neutral.

Cheeses
Cheese plays an important role in the diet of a vegetarian but not all cheeses are suitable. Vegetarians should avoid those that are made with animal rennet. If you are unsure which cheese to choose then look for ones that are clearly labelled 'vegetarian' cheeses. There is a good selection available including Cheddar, Double Gloucester, Red Leicester, Danish Blue and many delicious soft cheeses.

Soy Sauce/Shoyu
Naturally fermented soy sauce made from soya beans with wheat or barley is known as 'shoyu'. The manufactured soy sauce usually contains sugar and other additives. Shoyu makes an excellent flavouring for soups, stews, sauces and dressings and as it is quite salty allows you to cut down on added salt. Soy sauce can be used but the flavour will not be as strong.

Tahini
Tahini is a sesame seed paste widely used in the Middle East. It is useful as a flavouring in dips and sauces and can be used as a binding agent in rissoles and nut roasts.

Tofu
Tofu is soya bean curd. Its high protein content makes it a nutritional substitute for meat, fish and dairy products. It is also rich in iron, calcium and B vitamins. Tofu is a versatile ingredient: it can be stir-fried, deep-fried, marinated and added to dressings and sauces. It is available from healthfood stores as lightly pressed 'silken tofu', and 'firm tofu' which is more heavily pressed. Regular tofu has a texture in between the two.

Yogurt
Yogurt is a popular fermented milk product. It is very easily digested, especially goats' milk yogurt, and people who are allergic or sensitive to milk are often able to tolerate yogurt.

ABOVE: *Brazil nuts, hazelnuts, cashews, pumpkin seeds, roasted sesame seeds, whole mixed nuts, safflower oil, corn oil, olive oil, sesame salt, sesame seeds.*
BELOW: *Soy sauce, tahini, tofu, yogurt.*

SOUPS AND STARTERS

Piping hot and wholesome, or light and delicate, a soup should stimulate the appetite yet be carefully chosen so that it balances with the main course dishes yet to come. A hearty vegetable or bean soup, for example, should be followed by a light omelette, cheese quiche or salad; whereas a light cream soup should be complemented with a more sustaining savoury bake or casserole.

This clever balancing act also needs to be considered when choosing a suitable starter – rich pâtés, savoury cheesecakes and quiches being balanced with feather-light main courses; and fruity cocktails and marinated vegetables weighted with more substantial main course choices.

The choice of soups and starters in this section is large but shouldn't just be thought of as beautiful beginnings to a formal meal. Consider them as mid-day or light meals, suppers and snacks or double-up on your selection to make a main meal choice. Mixed and matched with salads, breads, rice and pasta accompaniments they will suit a whole host of occasions. Many can be made well ahead and some can be frozen – freeze a few for emergencies and you won't fail to be delighted and grateful for their convenience.

CHILLED CUCUMBER AND MINT SOUP

1 tablespoon oil
1 large onion, finely chopped
2 cucumbers, peeled and chopped
1 potato, finely chopped
900 ml (1½ pints) vegetable stock
1 bouquet garni
salt
142 ml (¼ pint) carton single cream
2 tablespoons finely chopped mint
mint sprigs to garnish

Heat the oil in a pan, add the onion and cook until transparent. Stir in the cucumber and potato, then add the stock, bouquet garni, and salt to taste. Bring to the boil, cover and simmer for 20 to 25 minutes. Remove the bouquet garni and cool slightly.

Sieve or work in a blender or food processor until smooth. Pour into a bowl, stir in the cream and mint and chill for 2 to 3 hours before serving.

Serve garnished with mint sprigs.
Serves 4 to 6

CREAM OF MUSHROOM SOUP

50 g (2 oz) butter
1 small onion, chopped
250 g (8 oz) mushrooms, chopped
salt and pepper
25 g (1 oz) plain flour
450 ml (¾ pint) vegetable stock
150 ml (¼ pint) milk
142 ml (¼ pint) carton single cream
3-4 mushrooms, sliced and fried in a little butter, to garnish.

Melt 25 g (1 oz) of the butter in a pan. Add the onion and cook gently, stirring, until softened. Add the chopped mushrooms, with a little salt and pepper. Cook until softened.

Melt the remaining 25 g (1 oz) butter in another pan. Stir in the flour and cook, stirring, for 1 to 2 minutes, Gradually stir in the stock and bring to the boil. Cook, stirring, for 2 to 3 minutes, then add the mushrooms and onions. Purée the soup in a blender or food processor, or rub through a sieve.

Return to the pan and heat gently.

Bring to the boil, then stir in the milk and cream. Check the seasoning. Heat through without boiling. Serve garnished with the mushrooms.
Serves 4

COLD BEETROOT SOUP

375 g (12 oz) beetroot cooked
142 ml (¼ pint) carton soured cream
600 ml (1 pint) vegetable stock

Place the beetroot and half the soured cream in a blender or food processor and process until smooth. Transfer to a bowl and stir in the vegetable stock. Chill well.

Pour into individual bowls and stir in the remaining soured cream.
Serves 4 to 6

Chilled Cucumber and Mint Soup

LETTUCE AND WATERCRESS SOUP

25 g (1 oz) butter
1 onion, chopped
1 large potato, chopped
900 ml (1½ pints) water
2 vegetable stock cubes, crumbled
1 round lettuce
1 bunch of watercress
salt and pepper
142 ml (¼ pint) carton single cream
chopped chives or spring onion tops to garnish

Melt the butter in a pan, add the onion and fry gently.

Add the potato to the pan and cook for 2 minutes. Add the water and stock cubes, bring to the boil and simmer for 15 minutes.

Tear the lettuce into small pieces and add to the pan with the watercress. Bring to the boil, then remove from the heat.

Process in a blender or food processor in 3 or 4 batches and pour into a serving bowl. Season with salt and pepper to taste and leave to cool. Chill in the refrigerator until required.

Stir in the cream and sprinkle with chives or spring onion tops to serve.

Serves 4 to 6

NOTE: Crunchy lettuces are not suitable for this recipe.

YOGURT AND CUCUMBER SOUP

1 cucumber, peeled and chopped
salt and pepper
500 g (1 lb) natural yogurt
142 ml (¼ pint) carton soured cream
300 ml (½ pint) water
6 mint sprigs, chopped
TO GARNISH:
½ teaspoon paprika
25 g (1 oz) sultanas (optional)

Sprinkle the cucumber with salt and leave to drain.

Place the yogurt, soured cream and water in a blender or food processor and blend until smooth. Stir in the mint and cucumber and season liberally with salt and pepper. Transfer to a serving bowl and chill until required.

Sprinkle with the paprika, and sultanas if using, to serve.

Serves 6

Lettuce and Watercress Soup; Yogurt and Cucumber Soup; Cold Beetroot Soup

CHILLED LEMON SOUP

25 g (1 oz) butter
1 onion, chopped
25 g (1 oz) plain flour
2 large lemons
900 ml (1½ pints) vegetable stock
150 ml (¼ pint) milk
salt and pepper
TO GARNISH:
6 tablespoons double cream, lightly whipped

Melt the butter in a pan, add the onion and fry gently until translucent, but not brown. Stir in the flour. Thinly pare the rind from 1 lemon and add to the pan with the stock and milk. Bring slowly to the boil, stirring constantly, then simmer for 5 minutes.

Finely grate the rind from the other lemon and keep on one side. Squeeze the juice from both lemons and add to the soup. Cool, strain and season lightly with salt and pepper. Chill well.

To serve, pour into individual bowls, top each with a tablespoon of cream and sprinkle with the grated lemon rind.

Serves 6

NOTE: This soup can also be served hot: stir the grated lemon rind into the soup and serve with croûtons.

CHEESE AND CAULIFLOWER SOUP

15 g (½ oz) butter
1 onion, chopped
1 small cauliflower, broken into florets
600 ml (1 pint) vegetable stock
1 bouquet garni
salt and pepper
1 tablespoon cornflour
300 ml (½ pint) milk
125 g (4 oz) Danish blue, crumbled
chopped parsley to garnish

Melt the butter in a pan, add the onion and fry until soft. Add the cauliflower, stock, bouquet garni, and salt and pepper to taste. Bring to the boil, cover and simmer for 15 minutes; cool slightly. Remove the bouquet garni.

Sieve or work in a blender or food processor until smooth. Blend the cornflour with 2 tablespoons of the milk. Add to the purée with the remaining milk. Bring to the boil, stirring. Remove from the heat and stir in the cheese.

Pour into warmed individual soup bowls and garnish with parsley. Serve immediately.

Serves 4

COUNTRY VEGETABLE SOUP

50 g (2 oz) butter
1 onion, chopped
2 carrots, chopped
2 celery sticks, chopped
1 large potato, chopped
1 × 227 g (8 oz) can tomatoes
600 ml (1 pint) vegetable stock
1 teaspoon tomato purée
salt and pepper
TO SERVE:
chopped chives or celery leaves

Melt the butter in a large pan, add the vegetables and cook until soft. Chop the tomatoes and add to the pan with their juice, the stock, tomato purée and salt and pepper to taste. Bring to the boil, cover and simmer for 30 minutes.

Remove from the heat, cool slightly, then purée in a blender or food processor, or rub through a sieve. Return to the pan, bring to the boil and simmer for 5 minutes. Check the seasoning. Serve garnished with chives or celery leaves.

Serves 6

Chilled Lemon Soup

COLD CUCUMBER SOUP

1 large cucumber
3 × 150 g (5 oz) cartons natural yogurt
142 ml (¼ pint) carton soured cream
1-2 tablespoons finely chopped mint
mint sprigs to garnish

Peel the cucumber and grate coarsely. Mix with the yogurt, soured cream, and salt and pepper to taste. Chill for about 2 hours.

Stir in chopped mint to taste. Pour into chilled soup bowls and top with mint sprigs to garnish.

Serves 6

CARROT AND CORIANDER SOUP

25 g (1 oz) butter
1 onion, finely chopped
1 clove garlic, finely chopped
25 g (1 oz) plain flour
1.2 litres (2 pints) vegetable stock
500 g (1 lb) carrots
2 teaspoons ground coriander
150 g (5 oz) carton natural yogurt
salt and pepper
coriander leaves to garnish

Melt the butter in a large pan, add the onion and garlic and fry until soft. Stir in the flour and gradually add the stock, stirring until thickened.

Grate the carrots then add to the pan with the ground coriander and simmer for 30 minutes.

Cool slightly then purée in a blender. Pour into a clean pan, add the yogurt, and salt and pepper to taste and bring to just below boiling point.

Garnish with coriander to serve.

Serves 6

SPANISH TOMATO SOUP

500 g (1 lb) tomatoes, skinned and chopped
1 onion, chopped
1 small green pepper, cored, deseeded and chopped
1 clove garlic, crushed
1 tablespoon wine vinegar
2 tablespoons olive oil
2 tablespoons lemon juice
1 slice white bread, crusts removed
300 ml (½ pint vegetable stock
salt and pepper
TO GARNISH:
diced cucumber
croûtons

Place all the ingredients in a blender or food processor and blend for a few seconds until smooth. Turn into a bowl, cover and chill thoroughly.

Serve the diced cucumber and croûtons as a garnish, in separate dishes

Serves 4

NOTE: to make croûtons, fry small breadcubes in butter until crisp.

Spanish Tomato Soup

CARROT AND ORANGE SOUP

25 g (1 oz) butter
500 g (1 lb) carrots, sliced
1 onion, chopped
900 ml (1½ pints) vegetable stock
pinch of sugar
salt and pepper
grated rind of 1 orange
juice of 4 oranges
142 ml (¼ pint) carton single cream

Melt the butter in a pan, add the carrots and onion and cook for 10 minutes, without browning.

Add the stock, sugar, and salt and pepper to taste. Bring to the boil, cover and simmer for 1 hour or until the carrots are tender. Cool slightly.

Sieve or work in a blender or food processor until smooth. Pour into a soup tureen and stir in the orange rind and juice. Leave to cool, then chill for several hours.

Just before serving, stir in the cream.

Serves 6

VICHYSSOISE

50 g (2 oz) butter
2 large onions, chopped
4 large leeks, white part only
4 large potatoes, diced
1.2 litres (2 pints) vegetable stock
1 bouquet garni
salt and white pepper
142 ml (¼ pint) carton double cream
TO GARNISH:
2 tablespoons chopped chives
croûtons

Melt the butter in a pan, add the onions and cook, without browning, for 10 minutes.

Add the leeks and potatoes and toss well. Stir in the stock and add the bouquet garni, and salt and pepper to taste. Bring to the boil, cover and simmer for 30 to 40 minutes, stirring occasionally. Remove the bouquet garni and cool slightly.

Sieve or work in a blender or food processor until smooth. Pour into a soup tureen and leave until cool. Stir in the cream. Chill for 3 to 4 hours.

Garnish with chopped chives and croûtons before serving.

Serves 6

NOTE: Alternatively, reheat gently without boiling until hot. Ladle into soup bowls.

Carrot and Orange Soup; Vichyssoise

CELERIAC AND POTATO SOUP

500 g (1 lb) celeriac
2 tablespoons lemon juice
1 onion, sliced
2 potatoes, chopped
1 litre (1¾ pints) vegetable stock
1 bouquet garni
salt and pepper
4 tablespoons natural yogurt

TOPPING

50 g (2 oz) butter
1 onion, chopped
40 g (1½ oz) wholemeal breadcrumbs
3 tablespoons chopped walnuts
2 teaspoons celery seeds

Cut the celeriac into cubes and toss them in a small bowl of water with the lemon juice. Place them in a pan with the onion and potatoes, add the stock and bouquet garni and bring slowly to the boil. Cover the pan and simmer for 30 minutes. Discard the herbs and process the soup in a food processor or blender to make a smooth puree. Season to taste with salt and pepper and stir in the yogurt. Reheat gently.

To make the topping, melt the butter and fry the onion for 2-3 minutes. Stir in the breadcrumbs and walnuts and stir-fry until they are dry and golden. Stir in the celery seeds. Scatter over the soup just before serving.

Serves 6

BROAD BEAN SOUP

25 g (1 oz) butter
1 onion, chopped
1 celery stick, chopped
25 g (1 oz) plain flour
900 ml (1½ pints) vegetable stock
1.5 kg (3½ lb) broad beans in pods, or 500 g (1 lb) shelled weight
1 bouquet garni
salt and pepper
2 egg yolks

TO GARNISH:

4-6 tablespoons whipped cream
chopped chives

Melt the butter in a large pan, add the onion and celery and cook for 5 minutes, without browning. Stir in the flour and cook for 1 minute.

Gradually stir in the stock, then add the beans, bouquet garni, and salt and pepper to taste. Bring to the boil and simmer for 35 minutes or until the beans are very tender. Remove the bouquet garni and cool slightly. Sieve or work in a blender or food processor until smooth. Return to the pan.

Blend the egg yolks with 2 to 3 tablespoons of the soup. Reheat the remaining soup, then remove from the heat and leave for 2 minutes. Stir in the egg mixture until smooth.

Pour into individual warmed soup bowls. Top each with cream and chopped chives. Serve immediately.

Serves 4 to 6

Broad Bean Soup

CHEESE AND CELERY SOUP

50 g (2 oz) butter
2 onions, chopped
1 head of celery, chopped
1.2 litres (2 pints) water
2 vegetable stock cubes
½ teaspoon grated nutmeg
salt and pepper
125 g (4 oz) blue cheese, chopped
celery leaves, to garnish

Melt the butter in a large pan, add the onion and celery and fry gently until softened. Add 300 ml (½ pint) of the water and simmer for 1 hour.

Process in a blender until smooth, then return to the pan and stir in the remaining water and the stock cubes. Add the nutmeg, and salt and pepper to taste. Bring to simmering point and stir in the cheese.

Transfer the soup to warmed bowls. Garnish with the reserved celery leaves and serve immediately.
Serves 4 to 6

TOMATO AND CARROT SOUP

397 g (14 oz) can chopped tomatoes
2 large carrots, grated
1 small onion, finely chopped
300 ml (½ pint) vegetable stock
1 teaspoon oregano
grated nutmeg
salt
1 bay leaf
1 teaspoon brown sugar
1 tablespoon chopped parsley to garnish

Place the tomatoes and their juice in a saucepan. Add the carrot, onion, stock, oregano, nutmeg and salt to taste, bay leaf and sugar. Bring to the boil, stirring, cover and simmer for 30 minutes. Pour into a hot tureen and sprinkle with parsley.
Serves 4

LETTUCE SOUP

50 g (2 oz) butter
250 g (8 oz) lettuce leaves, shredded
1 onion, finely chopped
600 ml (1 pint) vegetable stock
salt and pepper
1 teaspoon sugar
croûtons to garnish
BÉCHAMEL SAUCE:
300 ml (½ pint) milk
1 onion
4 cloves
4 peppercorns
pinch of grated nutmeg
25 g (1 oz) butter
25 g (1 oz) flour

Melt the butter in a saucepan, add the lettuce and onion and cook gently for 10 minutes, stirring occasionally. Add the stock, salt and pepper and sugar. Simmer, covered, for 30 minutes.

Meanwhile, make the sauce. Pour the milk into a saucepan, add the onion stuck with the cloves, the peppercorns and nutmeg. Bring to the boil slowly, turn off the heat, cover and stand for 15 minutes. Strain.

Melt the butter in a small pan and stir in the flour. Cook, stirring, for 1 minute then gradually add the hot milk. Return to the heat and bring to the boil, stirring constantly.

Add the sauce to the lettuce, mixing well, and simmer for 10 minutes. Cool slightly, then purée in a blender or food processor until smooth.

Return to the pan and heat through or, if serving cold, chill. Check the seasoning and garnish with croûtons.
Serves 4 to 6

Lettuce Soup

WATERCRESS SOUP

1 bunch watercress
2 onions, sliced
900 ml (1½ pints) vegetable stock
grated nutmeg
salt and pepper
40 g (1½ oz) skimmed milk powder
few watercress leaves to garnish

Remove any coarse stalks from the watercress and chop roughly. Place in a pan with the onions, stock and grated nutmeg, salt and pepper to taste. Bring to the boil, cover and simmer for 20 minutes. Leave to cool slightly.

Place the soup in a blender or food processor with the skimmed milk powder. Blend until smooth then return to the pan. Bring to the boil, stirring, and cook for 1 to 2 minutes. Check the seasoning and pour into hot bowls. Garnish with watercress.
Serves 4

Watercress Soup; Bortsch

BORTSCH

2 teaspoons oil
1 onion, chopped
2 celery sticks, chopped
375 g (12 oz) beetroot, chopped
125 g (4 oz) white cabbage, shredded
900 ml (1½ pints) vegetable stock
1 tablespoon vinegar
salt and pepper
1 bay leaf
3 tablespoons water (approximately)
150 g (5 oz) carton natural yogurt

Heat the oil in a pan, add the onion and celery and fry until soft. Add the beetroot and cabbage, then stir in the stock, vinegar, salt and pepper to taste, and bay leaf. Bring to the boil, cover and simmer for 1 hour.

Leave to cool slightly, remove the bay leaf then purée in a blender or food processor or rub through a sieve. Return to the pan, adding just enough water to give a pouring consistency. Check the seasoning and reheat.

Pour into hot serving bowls and stir in a little yogurt. Serve immediately.
Serves 4

QUICK MUSHROOM SOUP

50 g (2 oz) butter
40 g (1½ oz) flour
600 ml (1 pint) vegetable stock
300 ml (½ pint) milk
250 g (8 oz) mushrooms, finely chopped
1 clove garlic, crushed (optional)
salt and pepper
1 tablespoon lemon juice
1 tablespoon chopped parsley
125 ml (4 fl oz) single cream
paprika to garnish

Melt the butter in a saucepan, then stir in the flour. Cook, stirring, for 1 minute, then gradually stir in the stock and milk. Bring to the boil, stirring constantly.

Add the mushrooms, garlic, if using, salt and pepper to taste, and lemon juice. Simmer for 5 minutes, then stir in the parsley and cream. Reheat gently; do not allow to boil. Pour into individual soup bowls and sprinkle with paprika.

Serves 6

LEEK AND POTATO SOUP

50 g (2 oz) butter
1 tablespoon oil
6 leeks, sliced
4 potatoes, sliced
1.2 litres (2 pints) vegetable stock
salt and pepper
pinch of grated nutmeg
175 ml (6 fl oz) single cream
chopped chives to garnish (optional)

Heat the butter and oil in a saucepan, add the leeks and fry for about 10 minutes or until softened. Add the potatoes, stock, salt and pepper to taste, and nutmeg. Cover and simmer for about 30 minutes or until the vegetables are tender. Cool slightly, then work in a blender or food processor until smooth or rub through a sieve.

If the soup is to be served hot, return to the saucepan, add the cream and heat through; do not allow to boil. Adjust the seasoning if necessary.

If serving cold, stir in the cream and chill. Check the seasoning and garnish with chopped chives, if liked.

Serves 6

MINESTRONE SOUP

2 tablespoons oil
1 carrot, chopped
1 onion, chopped
2 celery sticks, chopped
1.2 litres (2 pints) vegetable stock
1 bay leaf
1 leek, shredded
1 potato, chopped
1 × 227g (8 oz) can tomatoes
1 clove garlic, crushed
¼ cauliflower broken into florets
75 g (3 oz) conchiglie
salt and pepper
TO SERVE:
grated Double Gloucester cheese

Heat the oil in a large pan. Add the carrot, onion and celery and fry until just beginning to colour. Add the stock, bay leaf, leek and potato. Bring to the boil, cover and simmer for about 40 minutes.

Chop the tomatoes and add to the pan with their juice, the garlic, cauliflower, pasta and salt and pepper to taste. Simmer for 12 to 15 minutes, until the pasta is tender. Check the seasoning, spoon into individual soup bowls and sprinkle with the cheese.

Serves 6

Quick Mushroom Soup

ARTICHOKE WITH HERB MAYONNAISE

4 globe artichokes
salt
5 tablespoons Green Herb Dressing (see page 68)
4 tablespoons Greek-style yogurt

Trim the points of the artichoke leaves square with scissors and cut off the stalk to level the base.

Place in a large pan of boiling salted water and cook for 35 to 45 minutes, until one of the leaves can be pulled out easily. Place upside down in a colander to drain and cool.

Gently ease the outer leaves so that you can remove the centre purple-tinged leaves and the 'choke', which is inedible; take care not to remove any of the 'fond' underneath.

Fold the dressing into the yogurt and spoon a tablespoon into the bottom of each artichoke. Place on individual dishes and serve the remaining herb sauce separately.

Serves 4

ONION QUICHE

PASTRY:
500 g (1 lb) plain flour
250 g (8 oz) butter
6 tablespoons water
FILLING:
175 g (6 oz) butter
1.75 kg (4 lb) onions, sliced
6 eggs
175 g (6 oz) Cheddar cheese, grated
salt and pepper

Make the pastry as for Spinach Cheese Flan (see page 91). Divide into 3 equal pieces, roll out and use to line three 20 cm (8 inch) flan dishes or rings.

Melt the butter in a large pan, add the onions, cover and cook gently for about 30 minutes, until tender.

Remove from the heat and beat in the eggs, then stir in the the cheese and salt and pepper to taste. Divide between the flan cases and bake in a pre-heated moderate oven, 180°C (350°F), Gas Mark 4, for 30 minutes, until golden and set. Serve hot or cold.

Serves 30

Cheese Pots

CHEESE POTS

40 g (1½ oz) blue cheese
25 g (1 oz) butter, softened
50 g (2 oz) Cheddar cheese, finely grated
2 tablespoons milk
1 small clove garlic, crushed
1 teaspoon chopped chives
salt and pepper
parsley sprigs to garnish

Place the blue cheese and butter in a bowl and beat until thoroughly blended. Beat in the Cheddar cheese and milk. Add the garlic, chives and salt and pepper to taste.

Divide the mixture between 2 small serving pots or dishes and chill before serving. Garnish with parsley and serve with hot toast.

Serves 2

PEAR WALDORF APPETIZER

1 crisp lettuce, shredded
2 celery sticks, chopped
1 red pepper, cored, deseeded and sliced
50 g (2 oz) walnuts, broken into pieces
175 g (6 oz) seedless white grapes
2 large dessert pears, cored and sliced
6 tablespoons Yogurt Dressing (see page 69)
1 tablespoon chopped parsley, to garnish

Mix the lettuce with the celery, red pepper, walnuts, grapes and pear slices in a large bowl.

Add the Yogurt Dressing and toss to mix lightly.

Spoon onto 4 individual serving plates and sprinkle with the parsley to garnish.

Serves 4

MARINATED MUSHROOMS WITH PASTA

375 g (12 oz) button mushrooms, wiped
6 spring onions, chopped
1 tablespoon chopped thyme
200 ml (7 fl oz) grape juice
175 g (6 oz) dried penne
250 g (8 oz) seedless white grapes, halved
salt and pepper

Place the mushrooms, spring onions and thyme into a large bowl, pour over the grape juice and mix well. Cover and chill for about 3 hours, stirring occasionally.

Meanwhile, cook the pasta in boiling salted water, according to the packet instructions.

Drain and allow to cool.

Just before serving, stir the pasta, grapes and salt and pepper to taste into the marinated mushroom mixture. Serve lightly chilled.

Serves 4

NEW YEAR PÂTÉ

25 g (1 oz) butter
25 g (1 oz) plain flour
200 ml (7 fl oz) milk
125 g (4 oz) blue Stilton cheese
50 g (2 oz) walnuts, chopped
2 teaspoons chopped parsley
salt and pepper
2 teaspoons brandy or mayonnaise
walnut halves and parsley sprigs to garnish.

Melt the butter in a pan, add the flour and cook for 1 minute. Gradually add the milk, mixing well, bring to the boil, stirring constantly and cook until smooth and thickened.

Remove from the heat and crumble in the cheese. Stir until the cheese melts then add the walnuts, parsley and salt and pepper to taste. Add the brandy or mayonnaise to give the pâté a fairly soft spreading consistency.

Spoon into one large or 4 small ramekin dishes and chill thoroughly.

Serve garnished with walnut halves and parsley sprigs. Accompany with hot toast fingers.

Serves 4

RIGHT: *Marinated Mushrooms with Pasta; New Year Pâté; Pear Waldorf Appetizer*

HUMMOUS

125 g (4 oz) chick peas, soaked overnight
salt and pepper
2 tablespoons tahini
1-2 cloves garlic, crushed
juice of ½ lemon
2 tablespoons olive oil
TO SERVE:
few lettuce leaves
2 teaspoons chopped mint

Drain the chick peas, place in a pan and cover with cold water. Bring to the boil, boil for 10 minutes then simmer gently for 2 to 2½ hours until soft, adding a little salt towards the end of cooking.

Drain, reserving 125 ml (4 fl oz) of the liquid. Place the chick peas in a blender with the tahini, garlic, lemon juice, oil, reserved liquid, ½ teaspoon salt and ¼ teaspoon pepper. Blend to a soft creamy purée; check the seasoning. Arrange on a bed of lettuce and sprinkle with the mint. Serve with crusty bread.

Serves 4 to 6

EGGS FLORENTINE

250 g (8 oz) frozen chopped spinach, thawed
salt and pepper
4 soft-boiled eggs
CHEESE SAUCE:
25 g (1 oz) butter
25 g (1 oz) plain flour
300 ml (½ pint) milk or cream
175 g (6 oz) Cheddar cheese

Line a shallow ovenproof dish with the spinach. Season well with salt and pepper. Place the eggs on top.

To make the sauce, melt the butter in a pan and stir in the flour. Gradually stir in the milk or cream and cook, stirring, until thickened. Lower the heat, add two thirds of the cheese and stir until melted, then pour over the eggs. Sprinkle with remaining cheese.

Bake on the top shelf of a preheated moderately hot oven, 200°C (400°F), Gas Mark 6, for 15 to 20 minutes, until golden brown. Serve immediately.

Serves 2 or 4

Eggs Mornay: Omit the spinach and add 25 g (1 oz) fine fresh breadcrumbs to the cheese for sprinkling.

CHILLED SHERRIED GRAPEFRUIT

4 grapefruit
125 g (4 oz) demerara sugar
4 tablespoons sherry

Halve the grapefruit, loosen the segments with a serrated knife and snip out the core with scissors. Sprinkle 15 g (½ oz) of the sugar and ½ tablespoon of the sherry over each half.

Cover the grapefruit halves with clingfilm and chill for at least 1 hour before serving

Serves 8

Hummous

VEGETABLE SAMOSA

PASTRY:
125 g (4 oz) plain flour
¼ teaspoon salt
25 g (1 oz) ghee or butter
2-3 tablespoons water
FILLING:
1 tablespoon oil
1 teaspoon mustard seeds
1 small onion, minced
2 green chillies, minced
¼ teaspoon turmeric
1 teaspoon finely chopped fresh root ginger
salt
125 g (4 oz) frozen peas
125 g (4 oz) cooked potatoes, diced
½ tablespoon chopped coriander
1 tablespoon lemon juice
oil for deep-frying

Sift the flour and salt into a mixing bowl. Rub in the ghee or butter until the mixture resembles breadcrumbs. Add the water and knead thoroughly to a smooth dough. Cover and chill.

Heat the oil in a pan and add the mustard seeds. Leave for a few seconds until they start to pop, then add the onion and fry until golden. Add the chillies, turmeric, ginger, and salt to taste and fry for 3 minutes; if it starts sticking to the pan add ½ tablespoon water and stir well. Add the peas, stir well and cook for 2 minutes. Add the potatoes and coriander, stir and cook for 1 minute. Stir in the lemon juice. Cool slightly.

Divide the pastry into 8 pieces. Dust with flour and roll each piece into a thin round, then cut each round in half. Fold each half into a cone and brush the seam with water to seal. Fill the cone with a spoonful of filling, dampen the top edge and seal firmly. Heat the oil to 180°-190°C, 350-375°F, or until a cube of bread browns in 30 seconds. Deep-fry until crisp and golden. Serve hot or warm.
Serves 4

Vegetable Samosa

FENNEL-ORANGE SALAD

3 tablespoons raisins
2 heads fennel, sliced
3 oranges, segmented
3 spring onions, sliced
12 pecan halves
watercress sprigs to garnish
DRESSING:
4 tablespoons French Dressing (see page 68)
1 teaspoon grated orange rind
1 tablespoon orange juice

Mix the dressing ingredients together and soak the raisins in it for about 30 minutes.

Arrange the fennel and orange segments on 4 individual plates, scatter the spring onions and pecans over and pour on the dressing. Spoon the raisins into the centre and garnish with the watercress sprigs.
Serves 4

SAVOURY MUSHROOMS

3 tablespoons olive oil
4 shallots, chopped
4 tomatoes, skinned and chopped
4 peppercorns, crushed
6 coriander seeds
1 bay leaf
1 thyme sprig
salt
500 g (1 lb) button mushrooms
4 tablespoons dry white wine
2 tablespoons tomato purée
chopped parsley to garnish

Heat the oil in a pan, add the shallots and fry until soft. Add the tomatoes, peppercorns, coriander seeds, herbs, and salt to taste. Stir in the mushrooms and wine, cover and simmer for 10 minutes.

Transfer the mushrooms to a serving dish. Discard the herbs. Bring the cooking liquor to the boil and boil for 5 minutes until well reduced. Add the tomato purée and spoon over the mushrooms. Sprinkle with parsley and chill before serving.
Serves 4

MIXED CHEESE PÂTÉ

75 g (3 oz) Danish blue cheese
50 g (2 oz) Wensleydale or Cheddar cheese, grated
50 g (2 oz) Double Gloucester cheese, grated
2 tablespoons natural yogurt
4 tablespoons double cream
2 teaspoons chopped chives
2 teaspoons chopped parsley
¼ teaspoon mustard
parsley to garnish

Mash the Danish blue cheese until soft, then add the Wensleydale and Double Gloucester. Mix together with the yogurt and cream. Add the chives, parsley and mustard and mix until well blended.

Transfer to a serving bowl and chill overnight. Remove from the refrigerator 1 hour before serving and garnish with parsley.

Serve with rye bread, melba toast or crispbreads.

Serves 4 to 6

MUSHROOM PÂTÉ

375 g (12 oz) mushrooms
1 onion
125 g (4 oz) butter
4 tablespoons sherry
salt and pepper
parsley sprigs to garnish

Chop the mushrooms and onion. Melt half the butter in a small pan, add the vegetables and fry gently for a few minutes to soften. Stir in the sherry and cook, stirring, until all the liquid has evaporated. Season with salt and pepper to taste and leave until cold.

Purée in a processor or blender with the remaining butter until smooth.

Spoon into a dish and garnish with parsley. Serve with toast.

Serves 4

POTTED CHEESE

25 g (1 oz) sultanas
2 tablespoons dry sherry
250 g (8 oz) mature Cheddar cheese
125 g (4 oz) butter
pepper

Soak the sultanas in the sherry for 45 minutes until plump.

Chop the cheese in a food processor. Add 50 g (2 oz) of the butter and process until blended.

Stir in the sultanas and sherry and season to taste with pepper. Spoon into individual dishes.

Melt the remaining butter and pour over the potted cheese. Chill for 1 hour or until required. Serve with hot toast or salad.

Serves 4

MINTED PEARS

113 g (4 oz) carton cottage cheese
1 tablespoon freshly chopped mint
salt and pepper
1 × 411 g (14 oz) can pear halves, drained
few lettuce leaves
few mint sprigs to garnish

Mix the cottage cheese with the chopped mint and salt and pepper to taste. Divide the mixture between the pear halves. Arrange the lettuce on a serving plate and place the pears on top. Garnish with mint.

Serves 4

BLUSHING EGGS

8 hard-boiled eggs
62.5 g (2.2 oz) packet creamy soft cheese
75 g (3 oz) can tomato purée
1 tablespoon mayonnaise (approximately)
salt and pepper
1 small frisée or lettuce, shredded
olive slices to garnish

Halve the eggs lengthwise, scoop out the yolks and place them in a basin with the cheese, tomato purée and mayonnaise. Beat well to give a soft piping consistency, adding more mayonnaise if necessary. Season with salt and pepper to taste. Pipe this mixture back into the eggs.

Serve on a bed of frisée or shredded lettuce, and garnish with olive slices.

Serves 16

MELON AND GRAPEFRUIT STARTER

1 honeydew melon
500 g (1 lb) tomatoes
½ cucumber
½ × 539 g (19 oz) can grapefruit segments, drained
1 tablespoon snipped chives to garnish
DRESSING:
3 tablespoons lemon juice
6 tablespoons vegetable oil
salt and pepper

Quarter the melon, remove the seeds and skin, and cut the flesh into cubes. Skin and quarter the tomatoes; cut the quarters in half if they are large. Peel the cucumber and cut into cubes.

Mix together the melon, tomatoes, cucumber and grapefruit in a serving dish.

Shake the dressing ingredients together in a screw-top jar and pour over the salad. Sprinkle with chives and chill for 1 hour.

Serves 8

LEFT: *Mixed Cheese Pâté*

ABOVE: *Tomato and Herb Tarts*

TOMATO AND HERB TARTS

175 g (6 oz) plain flour
pinch of salt
65 g (2½ oz) Cheddar cheese
1 tablespoon grated Double Gloucester cheese
3 egg yolks
100 g (3½ oz) butter, softened
FILLING:
375g (12 oz) tomatoes, skinned and sliced
2 tablespoons each chopped parsley, basil and thyme
50 g (2 oz) Double Gloucester cheese, sliced

Sift the flour and salt onto a work surface. Make a well in the centre; add the cheeses, egg yolks and butter, and gradually work into the flour. Knead until smooth, form into a ball, cover and chill for 1 hour.

Roll out and use to line eight 8 cm (3 inch) tartlet tins. Chill for 20 minutes. Line with greaseproof paper and dried beans and bake blind in a pre-heated moderately hot oven, 200°C (400°F), Gas Mark 6, for 20 minutes. Remove the paper and beans and return to the oven for 5 minutes.

Layer the tomato slices in the pastry cases, sprinkling each layer with herbs. Top with the cheese. Return to the oven for 5 minutes, until the cheese is bubbling. Leave to cool in the tins. Serve cold.

Makes 8

Danish Blue Mousse

DANISH BLUE MOUSSE

2 teaspoons agar-agar or vegetable gel powder
150 ml (¼ pint) vegetable stock
50 g (2 oz) butter
2 onions, chopped
2 cloves garlic, crushed
3 tablespoons cornflour
300 ml (½ pint) milk
1 bay leaf
300 g (10 oz) Danish blue cheese, crumbled
2 egg yolks
2-3 tablespoons cream
1 tablespoon chopped parsley
salt and pepper
2 egg whites
TO GARNISH:
cucumber slices
parsley sprigs or rosemary

Dissolve the agar-agar or vegetable gel powder in the stock. Pour a little into the base of a 1.2 litre (2 pint) mould, arrange a few cucumber slices in the stock and leave to set. Keep the remaining stock warm so it doesn't set.

Melt the butter in a pan, add the onions and garlic and fry gently until soft but not browned. Remove from the heat, stir in the cornflour, then gradually stir in the milk. Add the bay leaf and cheese and bring to the boil, stirring.

Cool slightly, discard the bay leaf and beat in the egg yolks, one at a time. Sieve or work in an electric blender or food processor until smooth.

Stir in the cream, remaining stock, parsley, and salt and pepper to taste. Whisk the egg whites until stiff then fold into the cheese mixture. Pour slowly into the prepared mould and chill overnight, or until set.

Turn out onto a serving dish and garnish with cucumber and herbs.

Serves 6 to 8

DEVILLED EGGS

6 hard-boiled eggs
4 tablespoons mayonnaise (see page 69)
1 teaspoon curry powder
½ teaspoon English mustard
½ teaspoon tomato purée
TO GARNISH:
cress
chopped chives
paprika or cayenne

Cut the eggs in half. Remove and sieve the yolks into a bowl; keep the whites on one side. Add the remaining ingredients and mix well to a smooth, soft paste. Pipe or spoon the mixture into the egg whites and arrange on a serving dish. Garnish with cress, chives and a sprinkling of paprika or cayenne.

Serves 4 to 6

VARIATIONS: To the sieved egg yolks and mayonnaise add 50 g (2 oz) grated cheese or finely chopped red and green pepper.

PEARS WITH BLUE CHEESE DRESSING

2 ripe pears
2 teaspoons lemon juice
125 g (6 oz) Danish blue cheese
175 g (5 oz) carton natural yogurt
salt and pepper
TO GARNISH:
4 lettuce leaves, shredded
2 mint sprigs

Peel the pears, keeping the stalks on. Halve the pears. Carefully remove the cores, using a teaspoon. Brush the pears with lemon juice to prevent discoloration. Cream half the cheese until soft and use 25 g (1 oz) to stuff each pear. Add the yogurt to the remaining cheese and blend well. Season with salt and pepper.

Arrange the lettuce on 2 small plates and stand a pear on each. Carefully coat with the cheese dressing and garnish with mint leaves.

Serves 2

CURRY CHOUX BALLS

CHOUX PASTRY:
40 g (1½ oz) butter
150 ml (¼ pint) water
50 g (2 oz) plain flour, sifted
2 eggs, beaten
FILLING:
250 g (8 oz) cottage cheese, sieved
4 tablespoons natural yogurt
curry paste to taste
1 tablespoon chopped parsley
TO GARNISH:
few lettuce leaves
watercress

Place the butter and water in a saucepan and heat gently until the fat has melted and the liquid comes to the boil. Remove from the heat and quickly beat in the flour. Continue beating over a low heat until the mixture leaves the sides of the pan. Cool slightly, then beat in the eggs, a little at a time.

Spoon the mixture into a piping bag, fitted with a 1 cm (½ inch) plain nozzle, and pipe 15 to 20 small bun shapes on to a greased baking sheet. Bake in a preheated hot oven, 220°C (425°F), Gas Mark 7, for 10 minutes, then lower the heat to 180°C (350°F), Gas Mark 4, and cook for a further 15 minutes. Make a slit in the side of each choux ball. Cool on a wire rack.

Mix the filling ingredients in a bowl. Halve the choux balls and spoon in the filling. Serve garnished with lettuce and watercress.

Makes 15 to 20

SAVOURY CHOUX BALLS

Choux pastry balls make delicious cocktail bites but ideally should be made and filled on the day otherwise they become soggy. Experiment with different fillings for variety:
*Cheesy – cream 75 g (3 oz) full-fat soft or cream cheese with 1 small clove garlic, 25 g (1 oz) butter and ½ teaspoon lemon juice. Add 25 g (1 oz) blue cheese and mix well.
*Pepper – cream 75 g (3 oz) full-fat soft or cream cheese with 1 small clove garlic, 1 deseeded and chopped red pepper, 2 teaspoons parsley and salt and pepper to taste.
*Green Goddess – cream 75 g (3 oz) full-fat soft or cream cheese with 2 tablespoons chopped spring onions, 1 tablespoon chopped parsley, 2 teaspoons snipped chives and 1 teaspoon chopped gherkins

BROCCOLI PANCAKES WITH LEMON SAUCE

500 g (1 lb) broccoli spears
1 onion, quartered
5 eggs
25 g (1 oz) wholemeal flour
salt and pepper
oil for shallow frying
SAUCE:
1 tablespoon lemon juice
1 tablespoon water
1 teaspoon cider vinegar
6 black peppercorns
4 egg yolks
250 g (8 oz) butter, diced
TO GARNISH:
1 lemon, quartered
4 small sprigs parsley, flat leaved type if available

Place the broccoli and onion in a steamer over a pan of boiling salted water. Cover and steam for 10 minutes, or until the broccoli is just tender. Plunge the vegetables in cold water, then drain them.

Place the broccoli, onion, eggs, flour, pepper and salt in a blender or food processor and process for a few seconds until the vegetables are coarsley chopped but not puréed. Set the mixture aside.

To make the sauce, put the lemon juice, water and vinegar in a small pan with the peppercorns. Bring to the boil and continue boiling until the liquid has been reduced by two-thirds, and only 1 tablespoon remains. Strain the mixture into the top of a double boiler or a bowl fitted over a pan of simmering water. Discard the peppercorns. Whisk in the egg yolks, and then the butter, a little at a time. Continue whisking until all the butter has melted and the sauce has thickened. Cover the surface closely with a piece of wetted greaseproof paper to prevent a skin forming on top. Stand the pan in a larger pan of hot water to keep the sauce warm.

To cook the pancakes, heat a little oil in a frying pan. Drop 2 tablespoon portions of the mixture, well apart in the pan. Cook for 2-3 minutes until the undersides are brown, then flip over the pancakes and cook the other sides. Keep the first batch warm while you cook the remainder.

Serve the pancakes garnished with lemon slices and parsley, and pass the warm sauce separately.

Serves 4

LEEKS À LA GRECQUE

375 g (12 oz) leeks
juice of ½ lemon
1 tablespoon oil
1 tablespoon water
1 clove garlic, crushed
3 tomatoes, skinned and chopped
salt and pepper
chopped parsley to garnish

Remove the outer leaves from the leeks and cut into 2.5 cm (1 inch) lengths. Wash thoroughly. Place in a pan with the remaining ingredients, adding salt and pepper to taste.

Heat gently to simmering point, then simmer for 20 minutes. Leave to cool in the liquid, then place in a serving dish and garnish with parsley.

Serves 4

TANGY GRAPEFRUIT

2 large grapefruit, halved
½ green pepper, cored deseeded and chopped
1 carrot, grated
2.5 cm (1 inch) piece of cucumber, diced
black pepper

Loosen the grapefruit from the skin and remove, leaving the empty half grapefruit shells intact. Scallop the edges of the shells if wished.

Remove the pith from the fruit, then chop and place in a bowl with the juice. Add the remaining ingredients, with pepper to taste, and mix well. Place in the refrigerator until required.

Just before serving, pile the mixture into the grapefruit shells.

Serves 4

CHEESE AND FRUIT COCKTAIL

2 dessert apples
lemon juice
2 celery sticks, chopped
50 g (2 oz) Edam cheese, diced
125 g (4 oz) grapes, halved and deseeded
½ lettuce, shredded
grated rind and juice of 1 orange
2 tablespoons natural yogurt

Chop the apples, place in a bowl and sprinkle with lemon juice. Add the celery, cheese and grapes and mix together. Place a little shredded lettuce in the base of 4 dishes. Pile the cheese and fruit mixture on top.

Mix the orange rind, juice and yogurt together, then pour a little over each cocktail. Serve chilled.

Serves 4

CORN-ON-THE-COB

4 fresh corn cobs
1 tablespoon sugar
TO SERVE:
salt and pepper
125 g (4 oz) butter
ground paprika (optional)

Strip the husks off the corn and remove all the silky threads. Place in a large shallow saucepan containing just enough boiling water to cover them. Add the sugar. (Do not add salt during cooking as this tends to toughen corn.) Return to the boil and boil for 5 to 6 minutes until tender. Drain thoroughly.

Place the cobs on individual serving dishes and insert special cob holders, small skewers or strong cocktail sticks at either end of each one for holding. Serve immediately with plenty of salt, pepper and butter. Sprinkle with a little ground paprika if liked.

CRUNCHY STUFFED PEARS

2 dessert pears
lemon juice
125 g (4 oz) cottage cheese
25 g (1 oz) walnuts, chopped
25 g (1 oz) raisins
½ red dessert apple, grated
1 teaspoon fruit pickle or chutney
salt and pepper

Cut the pears in half, remove the core and sprinkle with lemon juice. Place the remaining ingredients in a bowl, adding fruit pickle or chutney, salt and pepper to taste; mix well. Pile the mixture into the pear halves, place each one on a lettuce leaf and garnish with lettuce and tomato.

Serves 4

LEFT: *Leeks à la Grecque; Tangy Grapefruit*

RIGHT: *Corn-on-the-Cob*

VEGETABLES

It may seem odd to consider vegetable accompaniments in terms of vegetarian meals but not if you consider them as part of a main course assembly of dishes. A main-course vegetable and pasta, potato or rice dish can be served with one or two vegetable accompaniments; or four or five vegetable selections from this chapter can be cooked and served together to provide a main course. A plain boiled green vegetable with a stuffed and baked speciality, crispy-fried selection and gratinéed choice couldn't fail to delight a gathering of non-meat eating diners. So go ahead choose an exciting menu or accompaniment from this chapter, but do remember if you are preparing a simple vegetable accompaniment to serve it with, or precede it by, a protein rich dish.

There are few hard and fast rules about vegetable cooking, mainly because of the vast number of ways in which they can be cooked. There are however two which should be strictly adhered to. Never over-cook vegetables – not only are they unappetising but they lose some of their nutritional value; and never throw away the cooking liquid. Use as a stock for cooking soups, sauces, rice and pasta.

CELERY WITH WALNUTS

1 × 400 g (14 oz) can celery hearts
25 g (1 oz) butter
25 g (1 oz) walnut pieces

Place the celery hearts, with their juice, in a saucepan over moderate heat. When hot, drain, place in a warmed serving dish and keep hot.

Melt the butter in a small pan, add the walnuts and fry until just beginning to brown. Spoon over the celery and serve immediately.

Serves 4

DUCHESSE POTATOES

750 g (1½ lb) potatoes, boiled
75 g (3 oz) butter
1 egg, beaten
salt and pepper

Sieve or mash the potatoes and beat together with the butter, egg, and salt and pepper to taste. Put in a piping bag fitted with a large star nozzle and pipe into whirls on a baking sheet. Cook in a preheated moderately hot oven, 200°C (400°F), Gas Mark 6, for 20 minutes until crisp and golden.

Serves 6

COURGETTE CHIPS

500 g (1 lb) courgettes
50 g (2 oz) plain flour
salt and pepper
oil for deep-frying

Cut the courgettes into chips. Season the flour with salt and pepper and put in a large polythene bag. Add the courgette chips and shake to coat well.

Heat the oil in a deep pan to 180°-190°C, 350°-375°F, or until a cube of bread browns in 30 seconds, and fry the courgettes, in batches for 5 minutes. Drain on kitchen paper; keep warm while cooking the remainder.

Just before serving, plunge once again into hot oil for 1 minute. Shake off the excess oil and serve immediately.

Serves 6

BROCCOLI WITH HOLLANDAISE

1 kg (2 lb) broccoli
salt and pepper
3 egg yolks
1 teaspoon caster sugar
1 tablespoon white wine vinegar warmed
2 tablespoons lemon juice, warmed
175 g (6 oz) butter, melted

Cook the broccoli in boiling salted water for 10 minutes. Drain, place in a warmed serving dish and keep hot.

Put the egg yolks, sugar and a pinch each of salt and pepper in a blender. Work on high speed, trickling in the vinegar and lemon juice after 5 seconds. When absorbed, trickle in the warm melted butter, still on high speed.

Alternatively, put the egg yolks, sugar, salt and pepper in a basin over a pan of hot water. Stir in the vinegar and lemon juice, then gradually whisk in the warm melted butter.

Pour the sauce over the broccoli to serve.

Serves 6

LEFT: *Duchesse Potatoes; Courgette Chips*

RIGHT: *Fennel au Gratin; Broccoli Soufflé*

FENNEL AU GRATIN

2 fennel bulbs, sliced
salt
25 g (1 oz) butter
25 g (1 oz) plain flour
150 ml (¼ pint) milk
1 teaspoon coarse-grain mustard
75 g (3 oz) Cheddar cheese, grated
1 tablespoon breadcrumbs, browned

Cook the fennel in boiling salted water for 5 minutes. Drain, reserving 150 ml (¼ pint) of the cooking liquor. Melt the butter in a small pan and stir in the flour. Add the milk gradually, stirring constantly, and pour in the reserved stock. Simmer for 2 minutes, then stir in the mustard and all but 2 tablespoons of the cheese. Place the fennel in an ovenproof dish and pour over the sauce.

Sprinkle with the remaining cheese and the breadcrumbs and place under a preheated hot grill until browned. Serve immediately.

Serves 4

BROCCOLI SOUFFLÉ

375 g (12 oz) broccoli
salt and pepper
25 g (1 oz) butter
25 g (1 oz) plain flour
150 ml (¼ pint) milk
4 eggs, separated

Cook the broccoli in boiling salted water for 10 minutes, drain. Put the broccoli in a food processor or blender and process for 10 seconds.

Melt the butter in a pan and stir in the flour to make a roux. Gradually stir in the milk. Bring to the boil, stirring, and cook until very thick. Cool slightly. Add the egg yolks, broccoli, and salt and pepper to taste. Whisk the egg whites until stiff, then fold into the mixture.

Pour into a buttered 1.2 litre (2 pint) soufflé dish and bake in a preheated moderate oven, 180°C (350°F), Gas Mark 4, for 1 hour. Serve immediately.

Serves 4

Watercress, Courgette and Tomato Salad (see page 62); Petits Pois Nests

PETITS POIS NESTS

375 g (12 oz) potatoes, boiled
25 g (1 oz) butter
2 tablespoons milk
1 egg, beaten
125 g (4 oz) frozen petits pois

Mash the potatoes with the butter, milk and egg. Pipe into small nest shapes on a greased baking sheet and bake in a preheated moderately hot oven, 200°C (400°F), Gas Mark 6, for about 20 minutes, until golden brown.

Meanwhile, cook the petits pois in a little boiling salted water for 2 minutes; drain.

Transfer the potato nests to a warmed serving dish and fill with the peas. Serve hot.

Serves 2

FRENCH BEANS WITH GARLIC

500 g (1 lb) green or dwarf beans, cut into 5 cm (2 inch) pieces
25 g (1 oz) butter
2 tablespoons oil
2 cloves garlic, sliced

Plunge the beans into boiling water for 1 minute; drain. Just before serving, heat the butter and oil and add the garlic. Fry for 1 minute then add the beans. Toss well and cook for 2 minutes, stirring frequently.

Transfer to a warmed serving dish and serve immediately.

Serves 6

BAKED SLICED POTATOES

1 kg (2 lb) potatoes, thinly sliced
125 g (4 oz) butter
salt and pepper
chopped parsley to garnish

Soak the pototoes in cold water to remove excess starch; dry thoroughly.

Butter a large, shallow ovenproof dish; melt the remaining butter in a small pan. Put a layer of potatoes in the bottom of the dish. Drizzle a little butter over and season lightly with salt and pepper. Repeat these layers, finishing with butter. Cover and cook in a preheated moderately hot oven, 200°C (400°F), Gas Mark 6, for 1 hour.

Sprinkle with chopped parsley and serve from the dish.

Serves 6

SWISS RÖSTI

1 tablespoon olive oil
25 g (1 oz) butter
1 onion, chopped
500 g (1 lb) small potatoes
salt and pepper

Heat the oil and butter in a shallow frying pan, add the onion and fry until soft.

Slice the potatoes then add to the pan with salt and pepper to taste. Mix with the onions, then press down firmly. Fry slowly until golden on the underside. Turn and cook the other side. Slide the rösti onto a warmed plate to serve.

Serves 4

GRATIN DAUPHINOISE

50 g (2 oz) butter
750 g (1½ lb) potatoes
salt and pepper
125 g (4 oz) Cheddar cheese, grated
1 egg
284 ml (½ pint) carton single cream

Use half the butter to thickly grease an ovenproof dish. Slice the potatoes. Cover the base with a layer of potato. Sprinkle with salt, pepper and cheese. Repeat the layers, finishing with potato and reserving the last layer of cheese.

Whisk the egg and cream together. Pour over the top and dot with the remaining butter and cheese.

Bake in a preheated moderately hot oven, 190°C (375°F), Gas Mark 5, for 1 hour. If necessary, brown under a preheated grill. Serve immediately.

Serves 6

INDIAN STYLE CARROTS

50 g (2 oz) butter
750 g (1½ lb) carrots, sliced
1 potato chopped
2 teaspoons cumin powder
½ teaspoon chilli powder
1 teaspoon ground coriander
½ teaspoon turmeric
1 teaspoon salt
chopped coriander or parsley to garnish

Melt the butter in a pan, add the carrot and potato and fry gently for 5 minutes. Add the spices, salt and 6 tablespoons water. Simmer, covered, for a further 7 minutes or until the water is absorbed. Serve immediately, sprinkled with coriander or parsley.

Serves 6

Swiss Rösti; Indian Style Carrots; Gratin Dauphinoise

MUSHROOM AND BROCCOLI STIR-FRY

2 tablespoons oil
175 g (6 oz) small broccoli florets
125 g (4 oz) baby corn cobs
1 large leek, chopped
1 yellow pepper, cored, deseeded and cubed
375 g (12 oz) closed cup mushrooms, quartered
3 tablespoons light soy sauce
1 tablespoon clear honey
2 teaspoons ground ginger
1 × 432 g (14 oz) can cannellini beans, drained

Heat the oil in a wok or large heavy-based frying pan. Add the broccoli florets and baby corn and stir-fry for 2 minutes.

Stir in the leek, pepper, mushrooms and stir-fry for a further 2 minutes.

Stir in the soy sauce, honey, ginger and cannellini beans. Cover and cook for about 3 minutes, until the beans are thoroughly heated through.

Serve immediately.

Serves 4

MANGE TOUT AND COURGETTE STIR-FRY

3 tablespoons oil
375 g (12 oz) mange tout
6 spring onions, sliced
2 courgettes, sliced diagonally
2 cloves garlic, crushed
1 tablespoon soy sauce
3 tablespoons lemon stir-fry sauce
2 tablespoons vegetable stock
salt

Heat the oil in a wok or large heavy-based frying pan. Add the mange tout, spring onions and courgettes and stir-fry for 1 minute. Add the garlic and stir-fry for a further 1½ minutes.

Lower the heat slightly and add the soy sauce, lemon sauce, stock and salt to taste. Stir well to mix the flavours then serve immediately.

Serves 4

CHINESE CARROT AND MUSHROOM STIR-FRY

2 tablespoons sesame seed oil
175 g (6 oz) carrots, cut into strips
1 green pepper, cored, deseeded and cubed
250g (8 oz) flat mushrooms, sliced
1 × 227 g (8 oz) can bamboo shoots, drained
2 tablespoons light soy sauce
2 tablespoons Hoi Sin sauce
2 tablespoons vegetable stock

Heat the oil in a wok or large heavy-based frying pan. Add the carrot and green pepper and stir-fry for 1 minute.

Add the mushrooms, cover and cook for 2 minutes, stirring occasionally. Add the bamboo shoots, then gradually stir in the soy sauce, Hoi Sin sauce and vegetable stock. Bring to the boil, simmer for 1 minute, then serve immediately.

Serves 4

Chinese Carrot and Mushroom Stir-Fry; Mushroom and Broccoli Stir-Fry; Mange Tout and Courgette Stir-Fry

CARAWAY CABBAGE

375 g (12 oz) red or white cabbage, shredded
1 small onion, chopped
½ teaspoon caraway seeds
salt and pepper
15 g (½ oz) butter
½ red pepper, cored, deseeded and sliced

Place the cabbage, onion and caraway seeds in a pan of boiling salted water. Cook for 5 to 10 minutes, drain and return to the pan.

Add the butter and red pepper and toss the ingredients over a low heat for 1 minute. Add salt and pepper to taste and transfer to a warmed serving dish. Serve immediately.

Serves 2

Caraway Cabbage

CHINESE VEGETABLES

1 tablespoon oil
1 onion, chopped
1 large carrot, grated
3 chicory heads, trimmed and sliced
5 cm (2 inch) piece of cucumber, chopped
2 tablespoons soy sauce
2 teaspoons lemon juice
½ teaspoon sugar
salt and pepper
125 g (4 oz) bean sprouts

Heat the oil in a large shallow pan. Add the onion and carrot and fry quickly for 1 minute. Add the chicory and cucumber and cook for a further 1 minute.

Stir in the soy sauce, lemon juice, sugar, salt and pepper to taste, and bean sprouts. Cook for 1 to 2 minutes and serve immediately.

Serves 4

BRUSSELS SPROUTS WITH CHESTNUTS

125 g (4 oz) chestnuts
500 g (1 lb) frozen Brussels sprouts
salt
25 g (1 oz) butter

Score the chestnuts around the middle and place on a baking sheet. Bake in a preheated moderate oven, 180°C (350°F), Gas Mark 4, for 10 minutes. When cool enough to handle, peel the chestnuts.

Cook the sprouts in boiling salted water for 3 to 5 minutes.

Meanwhile, melt the butter in a shallow pan. Add the chestnuts and fry briskly, turning, for 2 minutes.

Drain the sprouts and place in a serving dish. Add the chestnuts and butter. Serve immediately.

Serves 4

TO PEEL CHESTNUTS

Chestnut skins can be removed by baking or boiling. To remove by boiling, place a few at a time in a pan of boiling water. Boil for 4 minutes then drain. Protecting your hand with a glove or cloth, and using a sharp knife, peel off the shell and furry inner skin while the chestnuts are still hot.

SPINACH AND YOGURT

1 kg (2 lb) fresh spinach or 500 g (1 lb) frozen leaf spinach
150 g (5 oz) carton natural yogurt
1-2 cloves garlic, crushed
salt and pepper

Rinse fresh spinach thoroughly and cook in a covered pan, without additional water, until tender. If using frozen spinach, cook according to packet instructions. Drain and cool.

Mix together the yogurt and garlic and stir into the spinach. Add salt and pepper to taste. Transfer to a serving dish.

Serves 4

CURRIED MUSHROOMS

150 g (5 oz) carton natural yogurt
2 tablespoons mango chutney
6 tablespoons salad cream
1 teaspoon curry powder
salt and pepper
375 g (12 oz) button mushrooms, sliced
chopped parsley to garnish

Mix together the yogurt, chutney, salad cream, curry powder and salt and pepper to taste. Add the mushrooms and mix well. Arrange in a serving dish and chill for at least 2 hours before serving. Garnish with the parsley.

Serves 4

LEFT: *Caraway Cabbage*

RIGHT: *Spinach and Yogurt; Curried Mushrooms; Turkish Cucumber Salad (see page 61)*

CORN FRITTERS

2 eggs, separated
1 tablespoon plain flour
1 × 326 g (11 oz) can sweetcorn, drained
salt and pepper
25 g (1 oz) butter for frying

Whisk the egg whites until stiff. Mix together the egg yolks, flour and sweetcorn. Season with salt and pepper to taste and fold in the egg whites.

Heat the butter in a large heavy-based frying pan. When the fat sizzles, drop in tablespoons of the corn batter. Fry until set and lightly browned underneath. Turn with a palette knife and fry the other side until golden. Drain and serve immediately.

Serves 12 to 14

DEEP-FRIED ONION RINGS

2 large onions, cut into 5 mm (¼ inch) thick slices
300 ml (½ pint) fritter batter (see opposite)
oil for deep-frying

Separate the onion slices into rings; discard the small inside rings.

Drop the onion rings a few at a time into the batter and lift out with a skewer.

Heat the oil in a deep-fryer until a cube of bread turns golden and rises to the surface immediately it is dropped in the pan. Deep-fry the onion rings for 2 to 3 minutes, until crisp and golden brown.

Drain thoroughly and keep hot as for Potato Fritters (opposite) while cooking the remaining rings.

Serves 4 to 6

SWEETCORN PUDDING

325 g (11 oz) canned sweetcorn
450 ml (¾ pint) milk
3 eggs, beaten
1 small onion, grated
1 teaspoon sugar
15 g (½ oz) butter, melted
salt and pepper

Drain the sweetcorn. Mix together all the ingredients with salt and pepper. Turn into a greased casserole. Place in a roasting tin containing 2.5 cm (1 inch) water.

Cook in a preheated moderate oven, 180°C (350°F), Gas Mark 4, for about 45 minutes or until a knife inserted into the centre comes out clean.

Serves 4 to 6

POTATO FRITTERS

3 medium potatoes
300ml (½ pint) fritter batter (see below)
oil for deep-frying

Cut each potato lengthways into 6 slices, 3-5 mm (⅛-¼ inch) thick. Spear each slice onto a fork and dip in the batter to coat thoroughly.

Heat the oil in a deep-fryer until a cube of bread turns golden and rises to the surface immediately it is dropped in the pan. Deep-fry a few fritters at a time for about 5 minutes, until crisp and golden. Drain thoroughly and place in a warmed heatproof serving dish. Keep hot in a preheated hot oven, 220°C (425°F), Gas Mark 7, while cooking the remainder. Serve hot.

Serves 16 to 18

VARIATION: Grate or finely chop the potato and stir into the batter. Cook as above for 3 to 4 minutes.

SAVOURY VEGETABLE FRITTERS

Vegetable fritters make a welcome change to the usual boiled and baked vegetable offerings. Many vegetables can be coated in batter and fried to make fritters – potato slices, corn, onion rings, small whole mushrooms, diced aubergine and courgette strips for example. Wash and dry the vegetables then coat in the batter and deep fry in hot oil as above. Drain on absorbent kitchen paper. Serve while still piping hot.

BASIC FRITTER BATTER

Sift 125 g (4 oz) plain flour and a pinch of salt into a mixing bowl and make a well in the centre. Add 75 ml (3 fl oz) milk and an egg yolk and, using a wooden spoon, gradually mix in the flour. When the mixture becomes very stiff, gradually add a further 5 tablespoons milk, beating well to make a very thick batter. Stir in 25 g (1 oz) melted butter and fold in 2 stiffly beaten egg whites. **Makes 300 ml (½ pint)**

Corn Fritters; Potato Fritters; Deep-Fried Onion Rings

COURGETTES À LA GRECQUE

300 ml (½ pint) dry white wine
juice of 2 lemons
150 ml (¼ pint) water
5 tablespoons olive oil
1 thyme sprig (optional)
1 parsley sprig
1 bay leaf
½ teaspoon ground coriander
salt and pepper
500 g (1 lb) courgettes, thickly sliced
TO SERVE:
1 tablespoon chopped fennel (optional)

Put the wine, lemon juice, water, oil, herbs, coriander and a little salt and pepper in a saucepan and bring to the boil. Put the courgettes in a blanching basket and immerse in the boiling liquid. Bring the liquid back to the boil and boil rapidly for 1 minute, then remove and drain the courgettes. Simmer the remaining liquid until it is well reduced. Cool.

TO FREEZE: Put the courgettes in a foil dish and pour the liquid over them. Cover, place in a polythene bag, seal, label and freeze.

TO SERVE: Thaw, covered, at room temperature for 2 to 3 hours. Serve cold, sprinkled with fennel, if liked.

Serves 4

BROAD BEANS À LA GRECQUE

2 tablespoons oil
1 clove garlic, thinly sliced
1 onion, finely chopped
500 g (1lb) shelled broad beans
8 tomatoes, skinned, seeded and chopped
2 tablespoons dry white wine
1 tablespoon chopped parsley
1 bay leaf
salt and pepper

Heat the oil in a pan, add the garlic and onion and fry for 4 to 5 minutes, without browning.

Stir in the broad beans and toss well to coat in the oil. Add the remaining ingredients, with salt and pepper to taste. Bring to the boil, cover and simmer for 15 minutes or until the beans are tender. Remove the bay leaf and leave to cool.

Serve chilled, with brown bread.

Serves 4

NOTE: Frozen broad beans can be used: cook the tomato mixture for 10 minutes before adding them.

SEMOLINA AND POTATO GNOCCHI

500 g (1 lb) potatoes, boiled and mashed
salt and pepper
grated nutmeg
450 ml (¾ pint) creamy milk
75 g (3 oz) fine semolina
2 eggs, beaten
50 g (2 oz) Parmesan cheese, finely grated
50 g (2 oz) butter, melted
75 g (3 oz) Gruyère cheese, grated

Season the potatoes liberally with salt, pepper and nutmeg. Mix well and gradually beat in the milk.

Return to the saucepan and heat gently. Stir in the semolina and cook over a low heat, stirring constantly, until the mixture is very stiff and leaves the sides of the pan. Remove from the heat and stir in the eggs and Parmesan cheese. Turn into a greased tin, cover and leave overnight.

Cut the mixture into 2.5 cm (1 inch) squares and, with floured hands, roll into cork shapes. Cook, a few at a time, in boiling salted water for 3 to 4 minutes until they rise to the surface. Remove with a draining spoon and arrange in a greased ovenproof dish. Pour over the butter and sprinkle with the Gruyère cheese.

Bake in a preheated moderate oven, 160°C (325°F), Gas Mark 3, for 15 to 20 minutes. Serve hot.

Serves 4

RATATOUILLE

2 tablespoons olive oil
2 cloves garlic, crushed
2 large onions, sliced
2 aubergines, sliced
6 courgettes, sliced diagonally
1 green papper, cored, deseeded and sliced
750 g (1½ lb) tomatoes, skinned and sliced
salt and pepper
2 tablespoons tomato purée

Heat the oil in a pan, add the garlic and onions and cook for 5 minutes, stirring occasionally. Add the aubergines, courgettes and pepper and stir in the tomatoes. Season with salt and pepper to taste, bring to the boil and simmer for 20 minutes. Add the tomato purée and cook for 10 minutes. Serve hot or cold.
Serves 4 to 6

FILLED TOMATOES

2 large tomatoes
15 g (½ oz) butter
1 small onion, chopped
4 tablespoons fresh breadcrumbs
1 tablespoon horseradish sauce
1 tablespoon chopped parsley
salt and pepper
watercress sprigs to garnish

Cut a slice from the top of each tomato and scoop out the pulp.

Melt the butter in a pan, add the onion and fry until soft. Stir in the breadcrumbs, horseradish, parsley and chopped tomato pulp. Season liberally with salt and pepper.

Fill the tomato shells with the mixture and bake in a preheated moderately hot oven, 200°C (400°F), Gas Mark 6, for 15 to 20 minutes. Serve hot, garnished with watercress.
Serves 2

BAKED COURGETTES

15 g (½ oz) butter
1 small onion, chopped
250 g (8 oz) courgettes, sliced
1 large tomato, skinned and sliced
½ teaspoon dried oregano
salt and pepper
1 egg, beaten
50 g (2 oz) Gruyère cheese, grated
parsley sprigs to garnish

Melt the butter in a saucepan, add the onion and courgettes and fry for 2 minutes. Transfer to a shallow ovenproof dish and place the tomato slices on top. Sprinkle with the oregano and salt and pepper to taste.

Mix together the egg, cheese and salt and pepper to taste. Spoon over the tomato. Cook in a preheated moderate oven, 180°C (350°F), Gas Mark 4, for 15 to 20 minutes until the topping is golden.

Garnish with parsley. Serve hot.

LEFT: *Courgettes à la Grecque*
ABOVE: *Baked Courgettes*

Potato Pancakes

POTATO PANCAKES

500 g (1 lb) potatoes, grated into cold water
1 onion, grated
2 eggs, lightly beaten
25 g (1 oz) plain flour
¼ teaspoon grated nutmeg
salt and pepper
butter for frying

Thoroughly drain the potato and mix with the onion. Squeeze well together then drain, if necessary, in a colander, pressing well to remove any excess liquid. Transfer to a mixing bowl and add the remaining ingredients, with salt and pepper to taste. Mix well.

Heat a little butter in a large, heavy-based frying pan or on a hot griddle until sizzling. Drop dessertspoons of the potato mixture onto the hot surface and spread with the back of the spoon until flat. Cook slowly for 4 to 5 minutes, until crisp and golden brown underneath. Turn with a palette knife and cook the other side.

Turn onto a warm heatproof plate; keep hot in a preheated moderately hot oven, 190°C, 375°F, Gas Mark 5, while cooking the remainder.

Serve as soon as possible; these pancakes should be eaten crisp.

Makes about 15

GREEN PEPPERS AND BEANS

500 g (1 lb) runner beans
2 green peppers, cored, deseeded and chopped
2 onions, finely chopped
salt and pepper
dried thyme
40 g (1½ oz) butter

If the beans are large, cut in half. Make alternate layers of the vegetables in a greased casserole, beginning and ending with beans. Sprinkle each layer with salt and pepper and a little thyme and dot with butter.

Cover tightly and cook in a preheated moderate oven, 180°C (350°F), Gas Mark 4, for 1 hour or until the vegetables are very tender.

Serves 4

LEMON COURGETTES

500 g (1 lb) courgettes
50 g (2 oz) butter
grated rind and juice of 1 lemon
2 teaspoons chopped rosemary
salt and pepper

Cut the courgettes into very thin strips or grate coarsely. Place on a large piece of foil.

Cream the butter with the lemon rind, lemon juice, rosemary and salt and pepper to taste. Spoon over the courgettes then seal the foil parcel to completely enclose.

Bake in a preheated moderately hot oven, 200°C (400°F), Gas Mark 6, for 15 minutes.

Remove from the oven and shake gently to coat the courgettes in the savoury lemon and herb butter. Serve immediately.

Serves 4

RED CABBAGE WITH APPLE

1 kg (2 lb) red cabbage, cored and shredded
40 g (1½ oz) butter
1 onion, sliced
2 cooking apples, peeled, cored and sliced
3 tablespoons water
3 tablespoons wine vinegar
4 teaspoons sugar
salt and pepper
15 g (½ oz) plain flour
chopped parsley to garnish

Blanch the cabbage in boiling water for 1 minute, then drain well. Melt 25 g (1 oz) of the butter in a flameproof casserole. Add the onion and fry until softened. Add the apples and fry for a further 5 minutes. Remove from the casserole with a slotted spoon.

Make alternate layers of the cabbage and apple mixture in the casserole, beginning and ending with cabbage. Sprinkle each layer with water, vinegar, sugar, salt and pepper. Cover tightly and cook in a preheated moderate oven, 160°C (325°F), Gas Mark 3, for 2 hours, stirring occasionally and adding more water if necessary.

Blend the remaining butter with the flour to make a paste. Mix with a little of the liquid from the casserole, then stir this into the casserole. Cook gently on top of the stove until thickened. Garnish with parsley.
Serves 4

SESAME POTATOES

750 g (1½ lb) potatoes
salt
3 tablespoons wholemeal flour
pepper
1 egg
1 tablespoon milk
6 tablespoons sesame seeds
oil for shallow frying
TO GARNISH:
snipped chives or chopped parsley

Cook the potatoes in boiling, salted water for about 10 minutes, until they begin to soften. Drain them and cut them into 1.0 cm (½ inch) slices.

Season the flour with salt and pepper and toss the potatoes in it to coat them thoroughly. Beat the egg and milk in one saucer and spread the sesame seeds on another. Dip the potato slices first in the egg and then the seeds so that they are well coated on all sides.

Heat some oil in a frying pan and fry the potato slices in a single layer for 2-3 minutes on each side. Serve hot, garnished with the herb.
Serves 4

SCALLOPED POTATOES

8 potatoes, thinly sliced
1 onion, thinly sliced
6 tablespoons plain flour
salt and pepper
600 ml (1 pint) milk
4 tablespoons dry breadcrumbs
15 g (½ oz) butter, melted

Make a layer of about one third of the potato slices in a greased casserole. Sprinkle with one third of the onion and flour and season with salt and pepper to taste. Repeat these layers twice, then pour over the milk.

Mix the breadcrumbs with the butter and sprinkle over the top. Cover and cook in a preheated moderate oven, 180°C (350°F), Gas Mark 4, for 1¼ hours.

Remove the lid and continue cooking for 15 minutes or until the top is crisp and golden brown.
Serves 6

Scalloped Potatoes

LEEKS WITH MUSTARD SAUCE

750 g (1½ lb) leeks
salt and pepper
1 tablespoon cornflour
300 ml (½ pint) milk
1 teaspoon mustard
1 crispbread, crushed

Trim the leeks, cut in half lengthways and wash thoroughly under cold running water. Cook in boiling salted water for 10 minutes or until tender, then drain. Place in a shallow heatproof dish and keep warm.

Blend the cornflour with a little of the milk. Heat the remaining milk, stir into the cornflour, then return to the pan. Heat, stirring until thickened. Add salt and pepper to taste, and the mustard, then continue cooking for a further 2 minutes. Pour the sauce over the leeks.

Sprinkle the crispbread over the top and place under a preheated hot grill for 1 minute. Serve immediately.

Serves 4

SWEET AND SOUR RED CABBAGE

1 red cabbage, shredded
1 large cooking apple, peeled, cored and chopped
15 g (½ oz) butter
3 tablespoons wine vinegar
1-2 tablespoons water
15 g (½ oz) sugar
salt and pepper
1 tablespoon redcurrant jelly

Place the cabbage, apple and butter in a saucepan. Cover and cook over a low heat, stirring occasionally, until the butter has melted.

Add the vinegar, water, sugar and salt and pepper to taste. Cover and simmer for 30 to 40 minutes.

Stir in the redcurrant jelly, check the seasoning and cook for 10 minutes. Transfer to a serving dish and serve hot or cold.

Serves 4

BEANS WITH TOMATO SAUCE

500 g (1 lb) runner beans, sliced
salt and pepper
7 g (¼ oz) butter
1 small onion, finely chopped
3 teaspoons tomato purée
½ teaspoon sugar
150 g (5 oz) natural yogurt

Cook the beans in boiling salted water. Drain and keep hot in a serving dish.

Melt the butter in a pan, add the onion and fry until soft. Add the tomato purée, salt, pepper and sugar. Cook for 2 minutes, then stir in the yogurt. Heat gently without boiling then pour over the beans. Serve immediately.

Serves 4

LEFT: *Leeks with Mustard Sauce; Vegetable Casserole; Beans with Tomato Sauce*

RIGHT: *Sweet and Sour Red Cabbage; Stuffed Tomatoes; Peppers à Provence*

STUFFED TOMATOES

4 large tomatoes
25 g (1 oz) Edam cheese, diced
125 g (4 oz) cottage cheese
15 g (½ oz) walnuts, chopped
1 spring onion, finely chopped
1 teaspoon chopped parsley
salt and pepper
TO GARNISH:
lettuce leaves
watercress
cucumber slices

Cut the top from each tomato and scoop out the inside. Chop the pulp and place in a bowl. Add the Edam and cottage cheese, walnuts, spring onion and parsley. Mix well and season with salt and pepper to taste. Pile the mixture into the tomato shells and replace the lids.

Arrange the lettuce leaves on a serving plate and place the tomatoes in the centre. Garnish with watercress and cucumber slices.

Serves 4

PEPPERS À PROVENCE

1 tablespoon oil
2 onions, sliced
4 green peppers, cored, deseeded and sliced
1 clove garlic, crushed
1 × 397 g (14 oz) can chopped tomatoes
1 teaspoon mixed herbs
salt and pepper

Heat the oil in a pan, add the onions and fry until soft. Add the peppers and garlic and cook for 5 minutes.

Stir in the tomatoes and their juice, mixed herbs and salt and pepper to taste. Bring to the boil, then simmer, uncovered, for 15 minutes. Transfer to a serving dish and serve hot or cold.

Serves 4

VEGETABLE CASSEROLE

250 g (8 oz) swede, sliced
2 carrots, sliced
1 large onion, sliced
2 celery sticks, chopped
salt and pepper
grated nutmeg
1 × 397 g (14 oz) can chopped tomatoes
parsley to garnish

Lightly grease a 1.75 litre (3 pint) casserole. Arrange the vegetables in the dish in layers, sprinkling each with salt, pepper and nutmeg.

Pour the tomatoes and their juice over the top, cover and cook in a preheated moderate oven, 180°C (350°F), Gas Mark 4, for 1 to 1¼ hours. Serve hot, garnished with parsley.

Serves 4

SALADS

Light, crispy and green, flavoursome and fruity, crunchy and wholesome or a main meal classic; there are a whole host of salads in this chapter to accompany main meals, provide main meals or suggest a course in themselves. For salads have no special season, nor culinary boundary. Easy-to-make and toss green salads or mixed vegetable salads can be made at any time of the year with in-season ingredients – you choose the ingredients and nature will bestow the virtue of variety. Rice, grain and pasta salads make wonderful spring, summer, autumn or winter fare if mixed and matched with seasonal fruits, vegetables, nuts, seeds and a tasty dressing.

Apart from being appetising and often very easy to prepare, many salad ingredients are also rich in fibre, which is so important to a healthy diet.

Salad dressings enhance and complement the taste and textures of the salad ingredients. Use them imaginatively but remember to add only a short time before serving – wilted, long-dressed salads prove unappetising to the eye and palate.

FRUITY RICE SALAD

125 g (4 oz) long-grain rice
salt
3 spring onions, sliced
2 celery sticks, diced
4 tablespoons sultanas
75 g (3 oz) Ready-to-Eat dried apricots, chopped
1 tablespoon chopped parsley, flat leaved if available
3 tablespoons French Dressing (see page 68)
1 tablespoon orange juice

Place the rice in a pan of boiling salted water and cook according to packet instructions. Rinse thoroughly, drain and leave to cool.

Place the rice in a bowl and stir in the spring onions, celery, sultanas, apricots and parsley. Toss until the ingredients are well mixed.

Mix together the French dressing and orange juice. Pour it over the salad and toss well.

Serves 4

VARIATION: Use stoned and chopped dates or dried figs instead of dried apricots.

GREEN RICE SALAD

175 g (6 oz) long-grain rice
salt
½ cucumber, diced
4 celery sticks, diced
1 green pepper, cored, deseeded and diced
6 spring onions, sliced
2 tablespoons chopped mint
6 tablespoons Vinaigrette Dressing (see page 71)

Place the rice in a pan of boiling salted water and cook according to packet instructions. Rinse thoroughly and drain well.

Place the rice in a bowl while still warm and add the remaining ingredients. Toss thoroughly and transfer to a serving dish.

Serves 6 to 8

BROWN RICE SALAD

175 g (6 oz) brown rice
6 spring onions
1 red pepper, cored, deseeded and diced
50 g (2 oz) currants
50 g (2 oz) roasted cashew nuts
2 tablespoons roasted sunflower seeds
6 tablespoons Sweet and Sour Dressing (see page 70)
3 tablespoons chopped parsley

Cook the rice in boiling salted water for 30 to 40 minutes, until tender. Rinse and drain well. Chop the spring onions finely.

Transfer the rice to a bowl while still warm and add the spring onions and remaining ingredients. Toss thoroughly and transfer to a serving dish.

Serves 6 to 8

NOTE: Sweetcorn and diced green pepper may be added to this salad.

ABOVE: *Fruity Rice Salad; Green Rice Salad; Brown Rice Salad*

RIGHT: *Leek, Cucumber and Tomato Salad; Coleslaw with Peppers; Fennel, Potato and Radish Salad*

LEEK, CUCUMBER AND TOMATO SALAD

3 leeks
½ cucumber, peeled
250 g (8 oz) tomatoes, skinned and deseeded
2-3 basil or parsley sprigs, chopped
2 tablespoons French Dressing (see page 68)

Slice the leeks and cucumber and chop the tomatoes.

Place the vegetables in a salad bowl and sprinkle with the basil or parsley. Pour over the dressing and toss well to serve.

Serves 4

FENNEL, POTATO AND RADISH SALAD

500 g (1 lb) new potatoes
salt
3 mint sprigs
1 fennel bulb
1 bunch of radishes
3 tablespoons French Dressing (see page 68)

Cook the potatoes in their skins in boiling salted water, with one mint sprig added, for 15 to 20 minutes. Drain well.

Thinly slice the fennel and radishes and thickly slice the potatoes.

Strip the leaves from the remaining mint sprigs and chop.

Place the fennel, potatoes, radishes and mint in a salad bowl. Pour over the dressing while the potatoes are still warm and toss well.

Serves 4

COLESLAW WITH PEPPERS

175 g (6 oz) red cabbage
½ green pepper
½ red pepper
1 small onion
salt and pepper
6 tablespoons Mayonnaise (see page 69)

Slice the cabbage. Seed the peppers, cut in half lengthways, then slice.

Slice the onion, or chop coarsely.

Place the vegetables in a salad bowl and season with salt and pepper to taste. Add the mayonnaise and stir well to combine.

Serves 4 to 6

WARM POTATO SALAD

4 potatoes, cooked
3 eggs, hard-boiled
2 onions, chopped
1 small green pepper, cored, deseeded and finely chopped
1-2 tablespoons snipped chives
1 tablespoon chopped parsley
1½ tablespoons cider vinegar or lemon juice
1 clove garlic, crushed (optional)
1 teaspoon horseradish sauce
black pepper

Dice the potatoes and eggs while still warm. Place in a serving bowl and add the remaining ingredients, with pepper to taste. Toss lightly.
Serves 4

Warm Potato Salad; Rice Salad

RICE SALAD

175 g (6 oz) long-grain rice, cooked
1 green pepper, cored, deseeded and chopped
250 g (8 oz) tomatoes, skinned and chopped
1 × 326 g (11 oz) can sweetcorn, drained
2 tablespoons sultanas
1 small onion, finely chopped
2 sticks celery, finely chopped
2 tablespoons chopped parsley
French Dressing (see page 68)
salt and pepper

Mix together the rice, pepper, tomatoes, sweetcorn, sultanas, onion, celery and parsley in a large bowl. Add enough French dressing to moisten the mixture and season to taste with salt and pepper.
Serves 4

MUSHROOM AND BEAN SPROUT SALAD

375 g (12 oz) button mushrooms, quartered
6 tablespoons Vinaigrette Dressing (see page 71)
250 g (8 oz) bean sprouts
1 red pepper, cored, deseeded and finely sliced

Place the mushrooms in a salad bowl, add the dressing and toss well. Leave to marinate for 1 hour, stirring occasionally. Add the bean sprouts and pepper. Toss thoroughly before serving.
Serves 6

CAULIFLOWER AND SPRING ONION SALAD

1 small cauliflower, broken into florets
salt
1 bunch of watercress
4 spring onions, chopped
5 tablespoons French Dressing (see page 68)
1 tablespoon sesame seeds, roasted

Cook the cauliflower in boiling salted water for 3 minutes; drain and cool. Add the watercress, spring onions and dressing and toss thoroughly. Transfer to a salad bowl and sprinkle with the sesame seeds. Serve immediately.
Serves 6

GRILLED PEPPER SALAD

4 large red peppers
2 tablespoons black olives
2 tablespoons chopped coriander
1 clove garlic, crushed
5 tablespoons French Dressing (see page 68)

Grill the peppers under a preheated medium grill for about 20 minutes, turning them frequently, until the skins are black. Rinse them, then skin, core, deseed and thickly slice them. Arrange the peppers and olives on a dish. Mix the coriander and garlic into the dressing and pour it over.
Serves 4

SPANISH COLESLAW

250 g (8 oz) white cabbage, finely shredded
1 small onion, finely chopped
½ green pepper, cored, deseeded and chopped
½ red pepper, cored, deseeded and chopped
1 large carrot, grated
50 g (2 oz) grapes, halved and seeded
6 tablespoons natural yogurt
1 tablespoon Low Calorie French Dressing (see page 68)
salt and pepper
parsley to garnish

Place the cabbage in a bowl and add the onion, green and red peppers, carrot and grapes.

Mix together the yogurt and dressing; season with salt and pepper to taste. Add to the vegetables and toss thoroughly. Transfer to a serving bowl and garnish with parsley.
Serves 4

Spanish Coleslaw

CAULIFLOWER, AVOCADO AND BEAN SPROUT SALAD

Bean sprouts are sprouted mung beans. They are most often used in Chinese stir-fried dishes but they are delicious combined with other vegetables in salads. Bean sprouts are nutritionally highly valuable, because they are rich in vitamins B and C, and also contain plenty of protein.

250 g (8 oz) cauliflower, broken into tiny florets
salt
1 avodaco pear, halved, stoned, and peeled
6 tablespoons Green Herb Dressing (see page 68)
250 g (8 oz) bean sprouts

Cook the cauliflower in boiling salted water for 2 minutes; drain and leave to cool.

Slice the avocado into the dressing and toss thoroughly. Add the cauliflower and bean sprouts and toss until well coated. Transfer to a salad bowl.

Serves 4 to 6

GREEN SALAD WITH ROQUEFORT DRESSING

1 small Cos lettuce
½ cucumber, sliced
2 celery sticks, chopped
1 head of chicory, sliced

DRESSING:
75 g (3 oz) Roquefort cheese, crumbled
2 tablespoons milk
6 tablespoons soured cream
salt and pepper

Tear the lettuce into pieces and place in a salad bowl. Add the cucumber, celery and chicory. Toss well together.

To make the dressing, place the cheese in a bowl and add the milk. Mash until smooth, then blend in the cream, and salt and pepper to taste. Pour over the salad just before serving.

Serves 4

BEETROOT AND MELON SALAD

1 small Ogen melon
250 g (8 oz) cooked beetroot, skinned
5 tablespoons French Dressing (see page 68)
2 tablespoons creme fraiche
coriander sprigs to garnish

Halve the melon and remove the seeds. Using a melon baller, scoop the melon into rounds. Scoop the beetroot in a similar way.

Mix together the French Dressing and crème fraiche and, just before serving, toss the beetroot in it. Arrange the melon and beetroot in a dish and garnish with the coriander.

Serves 4

LEFT: *Cauliflower, Avocado and Bean Sprout Salad*

RIGHT: *Baby Onions with Capers; Celery Julienne*

BABY ONIONS WITH CAPERS

500 g (1 lb) small onions
3 tomatoes, skinned and chopped
1 tablespoon capers
2 teaspoons tomato purée
½ teaspoon soft brown sugar
2 tablespoons olive oil
2 tablespoons chopped parsley

Plunge the onions into boiling water and boil for 1 to 2 minutes. Drain, cool slightly, then remove the skins.

Return to the pan with the tomatoes, capers, tomato purée, sugar, vinegar and oil. Cover and simmer for 5 minutes, then stir in the parsley. Transfer to a serving dish and chill before serving.

Serves 4

AUBERGINE SALAD

2 aubergines
2 cloves garlic, crushed
1 onion, sliced
1 tablespoon chopped parsley
4 tablespoons natural yogurt
salt and pepper

Pierce the aubergines with a fork and grill them under a preheated medium grill for 20 minutes, turning frequently. Cool then peel and chop them. Mix with the remaining ingredients and transfer to a serving dish. Line the dish with frisée leaves if you wish.

Serves 4

CELERY JULIENNE

4 celery sticks
½ cucumber
salt
½ bulb of fennel
6 tablespoons Green Herb Dressing (see page 68)

Cut the celery and cucumber into julienne strips 4 cm (1½ inches) long. Place the cucumber in a colander, sprinkle with salt and leave to drain for 30 minutes.

Trim the stalks, base and tough outer leaves from the fennel. Cut in half then shred finely.

Dry the cucumber on kitchen paper and place in a bowl with the fennel and celery. Pour over the dressing and toss well. Transfer to a serving dish.

Serves 4

ENDIVE AND GRAPEFRUIT SALAD

1 medium endive
1 grapefruit
3 spring onions, chopped
2 tablespoons Low Calorie French Dressing (see page 68)

Wash the endive and divide into pieces. Peel the grapefruit, removing all the pith, and divide into segments. Place in a bowl, add the remaining ingredients and toss well.
Serves 4

SPINACH AND ONION SALAD

750 g (1½ lb) spinach
2 tablespoons olive oil
1 large onion, chopped
2 cloves garlic, crushed
salt and pepper
142 ml (¼ pint) carton single cream
grated nutmeg

Cook the spinach in a large pan, with just the water clinging to the leaves after washing, for 5 minutes. Drain thoroughly and chop.

Heat the oil in a pan, add the onion and fry until softened. Add the garlic, spinach, and salt and pepper to taste and heat through.

Season the cream to taste with nutmeg and pepper. Pour over the spinach and mix well. Leave to cool, then transfer to a salad bowl.
Serves 4

KIDNEY BEAN AND CHILLI SALAD

175 g (6 oz) red kidney beans, soaked overnight
6 tablespoons Chilli Dressing (see page 70)
125 g (4 oz) frozen sweetcorn, cooked
1 red pepper, cored, deseeded and chopped
2 tablespoons chopped parsley

Drain the kidney beans, place in a pan and cover with cold water. Bring to the boil, boil rapidly for 10 minutes, then cover and simmer for 1 to 1½ hours, until tender, adding a little salt towards the end of cooking.

Drain the beans and place in a bowl. Pour over the dressing and mix while warm. Leave to cool.

Add the sweetcorn and red pepper. Toss thoroughly. Transfer to a serving dish and sprinkle with parsley.
Serves 4 to 6

MIXED VEGETABLE SALAD

½ small cauliflower
125 g (4 oz) carrots, sliced
125 g (4 oz) green beans
salt and pepper
125 g (4 oz) sweetcorn
1 celery stick, chopped
DRESSING:
4 tablespoons natural yogurt
½ teaspoon horseradish sauce
½ teaspoon lemon juice
TO GARNISH:
chopped parsley

Wash the cauliflower and break into florets. Blanch the cauliflower, carrots and beans in boiling salted water for 5 minutes, then drain and cool.

Mix together the cauliflower, carrots, beans, sweetcorn and celery in a bowl.

Mix the dressing ingredients together and season with salt and pepper to taste. Add to the vegetables, toss and transfer to a serving dish. Garnish with parsley.
Serves 4

HAWAIIAN CARROT SALAD

3 tablespoons oil
1 onion, chopped
150 g (5 oz) long-grain brown rice
1 teaspoon turmeric
pinch of chilli powder
125 g (4 oz) green beans, sliced
175 g (6 oz) carrots, sliced
100 g (4 oz) canned pineapple pieces
3 tablespoons canned pineapple juice
1 tablespoon wine vinegar
salt and pepper

Heat 1 tablespoon of the oil in a pan, add the onion and rice and fry for 3 minutes. Add the turmeric and chilli powder and fry for 2 minutes. Add 400 ml (14 fl oz) boiling, salted water, cover and simmer for about 25-30 minutes until tender. Drain and allow to cool.

Cook the green beans and carrots in a little water until just tender. Drain and allow to cool.

Mix the remaining oil with 3 tablespoons of juice drained from the pineapple, the vinegar and salt and pepper to taste. Stir into the rice with the beans, carrots and pineapple. Serve lightly chilled.
Serves 4

Mixed Vegetable Salad; Kidney Bean and Chilli Salad; Endive and Grapefruit Salad; Spinach and Onion Salad

Red Cabbage Salad; Bean and Sweetcorn Salad

RED CABBAGE SALAD

1 red cabbage
1 cucumber
375 g (12 oz) tomatoes
375 g (12 oz) dessert apples
juice of 2 lemons
8 tablespoons olive oil
salt and pepper

Shred the cabbage finely. Slice the cucumber and tomatoes. Slice the apples, discarding the cores.

Put the prepared vegetables and fruit in a salad bowl. Whisk together the lemon juice, oil and salt and pepper to taste. Pour over the salad and toss well.

Serves 20

BEAN AND SWEETCORN SALAD

375 g (12 oz) dried red kidney beans
2 × 326 g (11 oz) cans sweetcorn, drained
1 large onion, thinly sliced
125 ml (4 fl oz) French Dressing (see page 68)
2 tablespoons chopped parsley to garnish

Soak the beans in cold water overnight. Drain, place in a pan, cover with fresh cold water and bring to the boil. Boil rapidly for 10 minutes, then simmer for 45 minutes. Drain and cool.

Place in a salad bowl, add the sweetcorn, onion and French dressing and toss well to mix. Sprinkle with the chopped parsley just before serving.

Serves 20

THOUSAND ISLAND SALAD

3 round lettuce
2 bunches watercress
1 cucumber
1 kg (2 lb) tomatoes
DRESSING:
500 ml (18 fl oz) jar mayonnaise
1 tablespoon stuffed olives, chopped
½ green pepper, cored, deseeded and chopped
1 small onion, grated
1 tablespoon chopped parsley
2 teaspoons tomato purée

Tear the lettuce into small pieces and the watercress into sprigs. Divide between 2 large salad bowls. Slice the cucumber and tomatoes and add to the bowls. Toss together well to mix.

Place the dressing ingredients in a bowl and stir well until thoroughly combined.

Transfer to a sauce bowl and serve separately.

Serves 20

LENTIL AND TOMATO SALAD

250 g (8 oz) lentils soaked for 1 hour
salt and pepper
6 tablespoons Tomato and Garlic Dressing (see page 69)
4 spring onions, chopped
4 tomatoes, skinned and chopped
2 celery sticks, sliced
1 tablespoon chopped parsley

Drain the lentils, place in a pan and cover with cold water. Add a little salt and simmer gently for 30 to 40 minutes until softened. Drain well and mix with the dressing while still warm. Leave to cool.

Add the remaining ingredients, seasoning with salt and pepper to taste. Mix together thoroughly.

Transfer to a salad bowl to serve.

Serves 6

SPINACH AND MUSHROOM SALAD

250 g (8 oz) button mushrooms, sliced
4 tablespoons French Dressing (see page 68)
250 g (8 oz) spinach leaves
4 spring onions, chopped

Put the mushrooms in a bowl, add 3 tablespoons of the dressing and toss well. Leave to marinate for 1 hour, stirring occasionally.

Wash and thoroughly dry the spinach. Remove the thick centre stalks and tear the spinach leaves into a salad bowl. Add the marinated mushrooms, onions and remaining dressing. Toss well to serve.

Serves 4

BUTTER BEAN AND CAULIFLOWER SALAD

125 g (4 oz) butter beans, soaked overnight
salt
1 small cauliflower, broken into florets
125 g (4 oz) button mushrooms, sliced
6 tablespoons Green Herb Dressing (see page 68)

Drain the beans, place in a pan and cover with cold water. Bring to the boil and simmer for 1 hour or until softened, adding a little salt towards the end of cooking. Drain and cool.

Cook the cauliflower in boiling salted water for 3 minutes; drain and cool.

Place the beans, cauliflower and mushrooms in a salad bowl. Add the dressing and toss well. Serve immediately.

Serves 6 to 8

Lentil and Tomato Salad; Spinach and Mushroom Salad; Butter Bean and Cauliflower Salad

TABBOULEH

Bulgar or Burghul wheat is parboiled wheat. It is eaten widely in Eastern Europe. Tabbouleh originated in the Middle East.

125 g (4 oz) bulgar wheat
50 g (2 oz) parsley
4 tablespoons chopped mint
1 onion, chopped
3 tablespoons lemon juice
4 tablespoons olive oil
3 tomatoes, skinned, deseeded and chopped
salt and pepper

Soak the wheat in cold water for 1 hour. Drain thoroughly, then place in a mixing bowl.

Chop the parsley finely and add to the wheat, together with the remaining ingredients. Season with salt and pepper to taste. Mix well to combine the ingredients and transfer to a serving dish.

Serves 6

SPLIT PEA SALAD

200 g (6 oz) split peas
5 tablespoons Tomato and Garlic Dressing (see page 69)
2 tomatoes, skinned and chopped
2 celery sticks, sliced
50 g (2 oz) bean sprouts
3 spring onions, sliced
salt and pepper

Cover the split peas with boiling water and leave to soak for 20 minutes. Drain, place in a pan and cover with cold water. Bring to the boil, cover and simmer for 30 minutes, until softened. Drain, rinse and place in a bowl. Pour over the dressing and mix while still warm. Leave to cool.

Add the remaining ingredients, seasoning with salt and pepper to taste.

Serves 4 to 6

CHINESE SALAD

175 g (6 oz) red cabbage, finely shredded
few Chinese cabbage leaves, shredded
125 g (4 oz) bean sprouts
2 celery sticks, chopped
5 cm (2 inch) piece of cucumber, cut into strips
DRESSING:
2 tablespoons salad cream
4 tablespoons natural yogurt
1 teaspoon soy sauce
salt and pepper

Place the red cabbage in a bowl and add the Chinese leaves, bean sprouts, celery and cucumber.

Mix together the dressing ingredients, with salt and pepper to taste, and add to the vegetables. Mix well and transfer to a serving bowl.

Serves 4

LEFT: *Tabbouleh; Split Pea Salad*

RIGHT: *Algerian Salad*

ORANGE PASTA SALAD

125 g (4 oz) conchiglie
salt and pepper
50 g (2 oz) canned red kidney beans, drained
½ green pepper, cored, deseeded and chopped
2 teaspoons chopped parsley
grated rind and juice of ½ orange
1 tablespoon French Dressing (see page 68)

Cook the pasta according to the packet instructions. Drain and rinse under cold running water.

Place the pasta in a serving bowl. Add the kidney beans, pepper, parsley and orange rind. Mix the orange juice with the French dressing and add salt and pepper to taste. Pour over the salad and toss well. Chill before serving.

Serves 2

CELERY, APPLE AND WATERCRESS SALAD

3 red-skinned dessert apples, quartered and cored
6 tablespoons Vinaigrette Dressing (see page 71)
1 small head of celery, thinly sliced
1 bunch of watercress, divided into sprigs
25 g (1 oz) walnut pieces

Slice the apples into a small bowl, pour over the dressing and toss well. Add the celery, watercress and walnuts, mix well, then transfer to a salad bowl.

Serves 6 to 8

TURKISH CUCUMBER SALAD

½ cucumber
150 g (5 oz) carton natural yogurt
salt and pepper
2 tablespoons chopped chives

Cut the cucumber into small cubes. Mix with the yogurt, salt and pepper to taste and 1 tablespoon of the chives. Transfer to a serving dish and sprinkle with the remaining chives.

Serves 4

ALGERIAN SALAD

1 cucumber, diced
1 small green pepper, cored, deseeded and diced
50 g (2 oz) green olives, pitted and chopped
1 tablespoon chopped coriander
2 tablespoons chopped mint
2 teaspoons wine vinegar
2 tablespoons olive oil
salt and pepper

Mix all the ingredients together thoroughly, seasoning with salt and pepper to taste. Transfer to a shallow serving dish.

Serves 6

GREEN AND WHITE VEGETABLE SALAD

50 g (2 oz) frozen green peas, thawed
125 g (4 oz) white cabbage, thinly sliced
2 celery sticks, chopped
1 small green pepper, cored, deseeded and chopped
½ onion or ½ leek, thinly sliced
125 g (4 oz) Brussels sprouts, quartered
125 g (4 oz) bean sprouts
4 tablespoons French Dressing (see page 68)

Mix all the vegetables together in a salad bowl. Pour over the dressing and toss well. Serve immediately.
Serves 4

SPINACH AND FENNEL SALAD

125 g (4 oz) small spinach leaves
1 fennel bulb
50 g (2 oz) walnut pieces
2 tablespoons French Dressing (see page 68)

Remove any thick stalks from the spinach and tear the leaves into a salad bowl.

Trim the leaves from the fennel and reserve. Slice the fennel and add to the bowl with the walnuts.

Just before serving, pour over the dressing and toss well to coat. Garnish with fennel leaves.
Serves 2

COLESLAW WITH PINEAPPLE

½ large white cabbage, finely shredded
250 g (8 oz) carrots, grated
1 onion, grated
1 × 439 g (15 oz) can pineapple slices
125 g (4 oz) raisins
300 ml (½ pint) Mayonnaise (see page 69)
salt and pepper
chopped parsley to garnish

Mix the cabbage, carrots and onion together in a large salad bowl.

Drain the juice from the pineapple, reserving 150 ml (¼ pint). Cut the fruit into small pieces and add to the bowl with the raisins.

Blend the reserved pineapple juice with the mayonnaise and season with salt and pepper to taste. Pour over the salad and toss well to coat.

Sprinkle with chopped parsley to serve.
Serves 15

WATERCRESS, COURGETTE AND TOMATO SALAD

½ bunch watercress
1 courgette, thinly sliced
2 tomatoes, sliced
2 tablespoons French Dressing (see page 68)

Mix the vegetables together in a salad bowl. Just before serving, pour over the French dressing and toss well to coat.
Serves 2

Green and White Vegetable Salad

CHINESE CABBAGE AND WATERCRESS SALAD

125 g (4 oz) Chinese leaves, shredded
1 bunch of watercress
4 oranges, segmented
5 tablespoons Mint and Honey Dressing (see page 71)

Put the Chinese leaves, watercress and orange segments in a salad bowl. Pour in the dressing and toss well. Serve immediately.
Serves 6

CELERY, APPLE AND SESAME SALAD

1 head of celery, thinly sliced
4 red-skinned dessert apples, cored and thinly sliced
4 tablespoons Vinaigrette Dressing (see page 71)
1 tablespoon sesame seeds, roasted

Place the celery and apple in a salad bowl. Pour in the dressing and toss well.

Just before serving, mix in the sesame seeds.
Serves 6

BROAD BEAN SALAD

500 g (1 lb) shelled broad beans
salt
juice of ½ lemon
1 teaspoon oil
3 tablespoons natural yogurt
4 tablespoons Mayonnaise (see page 69)
1 tablespoon chopped mixed herbs (parsley, thyme and chives)

Cook the beans in boiling salted water for 10 minutes, then drain and place in a bowl. Mix with the lemon juice and oil and leave to cool.

Mix together the yogurt, mayonnaise and most of the herbs. Pour over the beans and mix well. Transfer to a salad bowl and sprinkle with the remaining herbs before serving.
Serves 4 to 6

Chinese Cabbage and Watercress Salad; Celery, Apple and Sesame Salad; Broad Bean Salad

FRUIT COLESLAW

1 red-skinned dessert apple, cored and chopped
2 teaspoons lemon juice
125 g (4 oz) white cabbage, finely shredded
1 small carrot, grated
50 g (2 oz) dates, stoned and chopped
1 tablespoon sultanas
50 g (2 oz) green grapes, halved and deseeded
2 tablespoons natural yogurt
2 tablespoons Mayonnaise (see page 69)
salt and pepper

Place the apple in a bowl, sprinkle with the lemon juice and toss well. Add the cabbage, carrot, dates, sultanas and grapes.

Mix together the yogurt, mayonnaise and salt and pepper to taste. Pour over the salad and toss well. Pile into a serving dish.

Serves 2

CHEESE MEDLEY COLESLAW

125 g (4 oz) white cabbage, finely shredded
1 carrot, grated
1 celery stick, chopped
25 g (1 oz) Edam or Cheddar cheese, diced
25 g (1 oz) Double Gloucester cheese, diced
25 g (1 oz) Stilton cheese diced
2 tablespoons natura yogurt
2 tablespoons Mayonnaise (see page 69)
salt and pepper
chopped parsley to garnish

Place the vegetables and cheeses in a serving bowl and mix together.

Combine the yogurt and mayonnaise with salt and pepper to taste. Pour over the salad and toss well.

Sprinkle with parsley. Serve with crusty rolls and butter.

Serves 2

LEEKS VINAIGRETTE

6 leeks
1 tablespoon chopped capers
DRESSING:
2 tablespoons lemon juice
4 tablespoons olive oil
1 teaspoon caster sugar
1 teaspoon coarse-grain mustard
1 clove garlic, crushed
salt and pepper
1 tablespoon each chopped parsley and chives

Slice the leeks very finely and arrange in a salad bowl.

Put the dressing ingredients in a screw-topped jar and shake well. Pour over the leeks, add the capers and toss well. Chill for 1 hour before serving.

Serves 4

Cheese Medley Coleslaw

BEAN SPROUT SALAD

125 g (4 oz) bean sprouts
1 celery stick, chopped
1 carrot, grated
2.5 cm (1 inch) piece of cucumber, cut in strips
3 tablespoons raisins
1 tablespoon French Dressing (see page 68)
1 tablespoon natural yogurt
salt and pepper

Place the bean sprouts, celery, carrot, cucumber and raisins in a bowl.

Combine the French dressing with the yogurt. Season with salt and pepper to taste. Pour over the salad and toss well.

Serves 2

ONION AND AVOCADO SALAD

½ avocado pear, stoned
2 teaspoons lemon juice
3 crisp lettuce leaves, shredded
2 spring onions, chopped
1 red pepper, cored, deseeded and roughly chopped
25 g (1 oz) peanuts
2 tablespoons French Dressing (see page 68)
salt and pepper

Peel and slice the avocado. Place in a serving bowl and sprinkle with the lemon juice. Add the lettuce, spring onions, red pepper, peanuts and French dressing. Toss well and season with salt and pepper to taste. Chill before serving.

Serves 2

Bean Sprout Salad; Onion and Avocado Salad

RICE AND ARTICHOKE SALAD

175 g (6 oz) long-grain rice
salt
25 g (1 oz) butter
1 clove garlic, crushed
1 onion, finely chopped
50 g (2 oz) button mushrooms, sliced
1 × 400 g (14 oz) can artichoke hearts, drained
2 tablespoons chopped parsley
DRESSING:
2 tablespoons lemon juice
4 tablespoons olive oil
1 clove garlic, crushed
½ teaspoon sugar
½ teaspoon French mustard

Cook the rice in boiling salted water for 12 to 14 minutes until just tender. Drain well and allow to cool.

Melt the butter in a pan, add the garlic and onion and fry until golden. Add the mushrooms and cook for 2 minutes. Stir into the rice.

Cut the artichoke hearts in half and add to the rice mixture with the parsley.

Put the dressing ingredients in a screw-topped jar and shake well. Pour over the salad and mix well. Turn into a salad bowl and serve immediately.

Serves 4 to 6

CAULIFLOWER, MUSHROOM AND ONION SALAD

125 g (4 oz) button mushrooms, thinly sliced
juice of 1 lemon
1 small cauliflower, broken into florets
2 onions, finely chopped
salt and pepper
1-2 tablespoons olive oil
150 ml (¼ pint French Dressing (see page 68)
paprika to garnish

Sprinkle the mushrooms with the lemon juice and put into a salad bowl with the cauliflower and onion. Season to taste with salt and pepper.

Add the olive oil to the French dressing and pour over the vegetables. Leave to marinate for 30 minutes, stirring occasionally.

Just before serving, sprinkle with paprika.

Serves 4

BROCCOLI AND ALMOND SALAD

375 g (12 oz) broccoli
salt
50 g (2 oz) flaked almonds, toasted
1 small red pepper, cored, deseeded and thinly sliced
4 tablespoons Vinaigrette Dressing (see page 71)

Break the broccoli into florets and blanch in boiling salted water for 4 minutes. Drain and leave to cool.

Place in a salad bowl with the almonds and red pepper. Pour over the dressing and toss thoroughly.

Serves 4 to 6

LEFT: *Broccoli and Almond Salad*

RIGHT: *Cabbage, Carrot and Apple Salad; Tomato and Cucumber Salad*

GREEN SALAD WITH AVOCADO

1 lettuce
1 bunch watercress
½ cucumber, sliced
1 green pepper, cored, deseeded and sliced
1 avocado pear
2 tablespoons lemon juice
4 tablespoons olive oil
1 teaspoon sugar
salt and pepper

Tear the lettuce into pieces and place in a salad bowl. Divide the watercress into sprigs and add to the bowl with the cucumber and green pepper. Peel the avocado, halve and remove the stone. Cut the avocado into slices just before serving, add to the salad and toss well.

Whisk together the lemon juice, oil, sugar, and salt and pepper to taste. Pour over the salad; toss well.

Serves 8

CABBAGE, CARROT AND APPLE SALAD

2 crisp eating apples
juice of 1 lemon
½ white cabbage, shredded
250 g (8 oz) carrots, shredded
½ teaspoon dried oregano
150 ml (¼ pint) French Dressing (see page 68)

Peel and thinly slice the apples and coat thoroughly with the lemon juice. Place in a salad bowl with the cabbage and carrot and mix well.

Add the oregano to the French dressing, pour over the salad and toss thoroughly.

Serves 4

SALAD OILS AND VINEGARS

A good salad dressing can lift a salad from the ordinary to the luxury class. Good quality oils and vinegars are a primary consideration in their preparation. They also provide the cook with an opportunity to ring the changes since each oil and vinegar has its own flavour and characteristics. Try using grapeseed, olive, safflower, sesame or walnut oil instead of a vegetable blend; and balsamic, cider, sherry, garlic, fruit or herb vinegars instead of the usual wine or malt vinegar.

TOMATO AND CUCUMBER SALAD

6-8 tomatoes, sliced
½-1 cucumber, peeled and sliced
salt and pepper
1 teaspoon caster sugar
150 ml (¼ pint) French Dressing (see page 68)
½ teaspoon dried marjoram

Arrange the tomato and cucumber slices in a shallow serving dish and sprinkle with salt and pepper to taste and the sugar. Leave to stand for at least 10 minutes.

Pour over the French dressing and sprinkle with the marjoram. Serve immediately. This salad makes a delicious side dish to pasta dishes.

Serves 4

SOURED CREAM AND MUSTARD DRESSING

2 teaspoons made mustard
2 tablespoons lemon juice
½ teaspoon caster sugar
2 × 150 g (5.2 oz) cartons soured cream
salt and pepper

Mix the mustard, lemon juice and sugar. Gradually stir in the soured cream, and season to taste with salt and pepper. Store in an airtight container in the refrigerator. **Makes 300 ml (½ pint)**

YOGURT AND CURRY DRESSING

300 g (10 oz) natural yogurt
2 teaspoons lemon juice
2 teaspoons mango sauce
1 teaspoon mild curry paste, or to taste
salt

Mix the yogurt, lemon juice and mango sauce, add curry paste to taste, and season with salt. Store in an airtight container in the refrigerator. **Makes 300ml (½ pint)**

FRENCH DRESSING

175 ml (6 fl oz) olive oil
4 tablespoons wine vinegar
1 teaspoon French mustard
1 clove garlic, crushed
1 teaspoon clear honey
salt and pepper

Put all the ingredients in a screw-topped jar, adding salt and pepper to taste. Shake well to blend before serving.
Makes 250 ml (8 fl oz)

Mustard Dressing: Add 2 tablespoons coarse-grain mustard.
Garlic Dressing: Crush 4 cloves garlic and add to the ingredients.

LOW CALORIE FRENCH DRESSING

1 tablespoon olive oil
6 tablespoons vinegar
3 drops of liquid sweetener
½ teaspoon made mustard
salt and pepper

Place all the ingredients, with salt and pepper to taste, in a screw-topped jar and shake vigorously until well blended.
NOTE: Cider vinegar or wine vinegar should preferably be used.
Makes 100 ml (3½ fl oz)

GREEN HERB DRESSING

25 g (1 oz) parsley
15 g (½ oz) mint
15 g (½ oz) chives
1 clove garlic, chopped
150 g (5 oz) carton natural yogurt
125 ml (4 fl oz) oil
juice of ½ lemon
salt and pepper

Remove the stalks from the parsley and mint. Place the leaves in a blender or food processor with the remaining ingredients, seasoning with ½ teaspoon salt and ¼ teaspoon pepper. Blend for 2 to 3 minutes.

Store in an airtight container in the refrigerator. Shake well to blend before serving.
Makes 300 ml (½ pint)

YOGURT DRESSING

300 g (10 oz) natural yogurt
2 tablespoons lemon juice
1 clove garlic, crushed
salt and pepper

Place all the ingredients in a bowl, seasoning with ½ teaspoon salt and ½ teaspoon pepper. Mix together thoroughly. Store in an airtight container in the refrigerator.
Makes 300 ml (½ pint)

MAYONNAISE

1 egg yolk
¼ teaspoon each salt, pepper and dry mustard
150 ml (¼ pint) olive oil
1-2 teaspoons cider vinegar

Beat the egg yolk and seasoning in a bowl. Add the oil drop by drop, beating constantly. As it thickens, add the oil in a steady stream. Add the vinegar and mix thoroughly.
Makes about 150 ml (¼ pint)

TOMATO AND GARLIC DRESSING

300 ml (½ pint) tomato juice
1 tablespoon lemon juice
1 clove garlic, crushed
2 tablespoons chopped chives
2 tablesj oons olive oil
salt and pepper

Put all the ingredients in a screw-topped jar, adding salt and pepper to taste. Shake well to blend before serving.
Makes 300 ml (½ pint)

Mayonnaise; Green Herb Dressing; Tomato and Garlic Dressing; Yogurt Dressing

Stilton Dressing; Sweet and Sour Dressing

THOUSAND ISLANDS DRESSING

150g (5 oz) natural yogurt
1 tablespoon chopped black olives
1 teaspoon grated onion
1 hard-boiled egg, chopped
2 tablespoons chopped cucumber
2 tablespoons olive oil
pepper

Place the yogurt in a bowl and beat in the remaining ingredients, seasoning with pepper to taste. Serve chilled.
Makes about 300 ml (½ pint)
NOTE: For a richer sauce you can use mayonnaise (see page 69) instead of yogurt.

STILTON DRESSING

50 g (2 oz) Stilton cheese
150 g (5 oz) carton natural yogurt yogurt
1 tablespoon chopped chives
salt and pepper

Mash the cheese with a fork and gradually add the yogurt to make a smooth paste. Stir in the chives and season with salt and pepper to taste. Store in an airtight container in the refrigerator.
Makes 250 ml (8 fl oz)

SWEET AND SOUR DRESSING

150 ml (¼ pint) sunflower oil
2 tablespoons honey
3 tablespoons soy sauce
3 tablespoons red wine vinegar
salt and pepper

Put all the ingredients in a screw-top jar, season with salt and pepper to taste. Shake well to blend before using.
Makes about 300 ml (½ pint)

Chilli Dressing: Add 1 deseeded and finely chopped green chilli.

TOMATO DRESSING

150 ml (¼ pint) tomato juice
150 ml (¼ pint) vinegar
1 teaspoon grated onion
½ teaspoon dried mustard
1 teaspoon sugar
1 teaspoon chopped parsley
salt and pepper

Place all the ingredients, with salt and pepper to taste, in a screw-topped jar and shake vigorously until well blended.
Makes 300 ml (½ pint)

MINT AND HONEY DRESSING

2 tablespoons clear honey
4 tablespoons cider vinegar
3 tablespoons olive oil
1 tablespoon chopped mint
salt and pepper

Put all the ingredients in a screw-topped jar, adding salt and pepper to taste. Shake well to blend before serving.
Makes 150 ml (¼ pint)

VINAIGRETTE DRESSING

175 ml (6 fl oz) olive oil
2 tablespoons cider vinegar
2 tablespoons lemon juice
1 teaspoon muscovado sugar
1 clove garlic, crushed
½ teaspoon mustard
2 tablespoons chopped mixed herbs (mint, parsley, chervil, chives and thyme)
salt and pepper

Put all the ingredients in a screw-topped jar, adding salt and pepper to taste. Shake well to blend before serving.
Makes 250 ml (8 fl oz)

GINGER SOY DRESSING

175 ml (6 fl oz) olive oil
4 tablespoons soy sauce
2 tablespoons lemon juice
1 clove garlic, crushed
1 cm (½ inch) piece fresh root ginger, finely chopped
salt and pepper

Put all the ingredients in a screw-topped jar, adding salt and pepper to taste. Shake well to blend before serving.
Makes 300 ml (½ pint)

WATERCRESS DRESSING

1 small bunch watercress
2 × 150 g (5.2 oz) cartons soured cream
2 tablespoons olive oil
1 teaspoon lemon juice
salt and pepper

Discard the tough lower stalks of the watercress and finely chop the rest. Mix it with the remaining ingredients, and season with salt and pepper to taste. Store in a covered container in the refrigerator. **Makes 300 ml (½ pint)**

QUACAMOLE DRESSING

2 ripe avocados
2 tablespoons lemon juice
1 teaspoon chopped onion
4 tablespoons olive oil
pinch chilli powder
salt and pepper

Cut the avocados in half and remove the stones. Scoop out the flesh and process it in a blender or food processor with the lemon juice and onion until smooth. Pour on the oil in a thin, steady stream, processing until it is absorbed. Season to taste with chilli powder, salt and pepper. Store in a covered container in the refrigerator. **Makes about 300 ml (½ pint)**

MAIN COURSES

Novice vegetarians often find it difficult to break away from the meat-and-two-vegetable concept of menu planning, but it is really quite easy. Simply choose one or two main course dishes from this chapter and combine them with salads and vegetables that complement them in colour, flavour and texture. For example, you might try Cottage Cheese and Spinach Flan with Middle Eastern Rice, and Hawaiian Carrot Salad, or perhaps Aubergine Bean Bake, Greek Salad and Duchesse Potatoes, or Red Pepper and Lentil Croquettes, Noodles with Nuts and Green Salad with Stilton Dressing. Consider vegetable casseroles, pasta stews, savoury bakes and flans, curries, pancakes and hotpots. The selection of dishes is wide, the combinations endless. Menu building in this way will provide meals that are not only suitable for formal and informal entertaining occasions as well as for family meals, but will provide meals rich in all the essential nutrients for a healthy balanced diet.

TOFU STIR-FRY

2 tablespoons soy sauce
2 tablespoons dry sherry
2 tablespoons orange juice
2 spring onions, sliced
1 clove garlic, crushed
250 g (8 oz) tofu (beancurd), cubed
2 tablespoons sesame oil
25 g (1 oz) blanched almonds
1 red pepper, cored, deseeded and sliced
1 green chilli, cored, deseeded and sliced
175 g (6 oz) mange tout, halved
100 g (4 oz) button mushrooms, sliced
250 g (8 oz) bean sprouts
2 tablespoons sesame seeds, toasted

Mix the soy sauce, sherry, orange juice, spring onion and garlic in a bowl. Add the tofu, cover and leave to marinate for 1 hour. Drain, reserving the marinade.

Heat the oil in a wok or large frying pan. Add the almonds and stir-fry for 1 minute to brown them on all sides. Remove with a slotted spoon and set aside.

Add the tofu and stir-fry for 2 minutes until beginning to brown evenly. Remove with a slotted spoon and set aside.

Add the pepper, chilli and mange tout and stir-fry for 2 minutes. Add the mushrooms and bean sprouts and stir-fry for 1 minute. Return the almonds to the pan, add the reserved marinade and stir-fry for 2 minutes.

Stir in the tofu, taking care not to break it, and transfer to a warmed serving dish. Sprinkle with the sesame seeds to serve.

Serves 4

TOFU

Tofu, which is also known as bean curd and as tahu, is made from fermented soya beans and sold in the form of a soft, white block. It is widely used in Chinese and Indonesian cookery, particularly in vegetarian dishes.

It has little flavour of its own, and readily absorbs those of any other ingredients in a dish, especially strong-flavoured sauces such as soy. It can be cut into slices or cubes of any size, and does not shrink or crumble in cooking.

Store it in cold water in an airtight container in the refrigerator.

Tofu Stir-Fry, Vegetable Rice with Skewered Tofu, and Devilled Vegetable Rice with Tofu

VEGETABLE RICE WITH SKEWERED TOFU

5 tablespoons soy sauce
3 tablespoons white wine
3 tablespoons light brown sugar
1 teaspoon grated fresh root ginger or 1½ teaspoons ground ginger
3 cloves garlic, crushed
3 tablespoons sesame oil
¼ teaspoon mustard powder
750 g (1½ lb) tofu (bean curd), chopped
2 onions, thinly sliced
125 g (4 oz) mushrooms, chopped
1 small carrot, grated
375 g (12 oz) cooked long-grain brown rice
salt and pepper
2 tablespoons chopped parsley or spring onions to serve

Mix 3 tablespoons of the soy sauce with the wine, sugar, ginger, 2 cloves of the garlic, 1 tablespoon of the sesame oil and the mustard in a large bowl. Add the tofu, mixing well and leave to marinate for 1 hour or more.

Heat the remaining oil in a wok or frying pan, add the remaining garlic and onions and stir-fry for 2 minutes. Add the mushrooms and carrot and stir-fry for 1 minute. Add the rice, remaining soy sauce and salt and pepper to taste. Stir-fry for about 2 minutes until heated through. Keep warm.

Meanwhile, drain the tofu from the marinade and thread onto small skewers. Cook under a preheated hot grill for about 30 seconds until the tofu is speckled. Turn over and baste with the marinade and grill for a further 30 seconds until speckled.

Spoon the vegetable rice onto a warmed serving plate and top with the skewered tofu. Sprinkle with parsley or spring onions to serve.

Serves 4

DEVILLED VEGETABLE RICE WITH TOFU

250 g (8 oz) long-grain brown rice
375 g (12 oz) tofu (bean curd), cubed
4 spring onions or 1 small leek, very finely chopped
2 tablespoons chopped parsley
½ green pepper, cored, deseeded and sliced

DRESSING:

6 tablespoons oil
3 tablespoons wine or rice vinegar
1 tablespoon lemon juice
1 teaspoon curry powder
¼ teaspoon chilli powder
1 clove garlic, crushed
salt and pepper
tomato slices to garnish

Cook the rice in boiling salted water according to the packet instructions. Drain and allow to cool.

Mix the rice with the tofu, spring onions or leek, parsley and green pepper.

To make the dressing, mix the oil with the vinegar, lemon juice, curry powder, chilli powder, garlic and salt and pepper to taste, blending well. Add to the rice and tofu mixture and toss lightly to mix. Cover and leave to stand for 1 to 2 hours before serving to allow the flavours to develop.

Stir again just before serving to coat the rice and tofu in the devilled dressing. Garnish with tomato slices.

Serves 6

WHOLEMEAL CHEESE PUDDING

8 slices buttered wholemeal bread
75 g (3 oz) Double Gloucester cheese, grated
75 g (3 oz) Leicester cheese, grated
3 eggs
475 ml (16 fl oz) milk
1 teaspoon mustard
1 teaspoon caraway seeds (optional)
1 tablespoon chopped parsley
salt and pepper
TO GARNISH:
tomato slices
parsley sprig

Make sandwiches with the bread and Double Gloucester cheese. Remove the crusts and cut into triangles. Arrange in a shallow greased 1.2 litre (2 pint) ovenproof dish. Sprinkle with 50 g (2 oz) of the Leicester cheese.

Whisk together the eggs, milk, mustard, caraway seeds if using, parsley, and salt and pepper to taste. Pour over the bread and leave to stand for 30 minutes.

Sprinkle with the remaining cheese and bake in a preheated moderate oven, 160°C (325°F), Gas Mark 3, for 40 to 45 minutes, or until set and golden. Serve immediately, garnished with tomato and parsley.

Serves 4

VEGETABLE PIE

1 kg (2 lb) potatoes, cooked
50 g (2 oz) butter
150 ml (¼ pint) milk
250 g (8 oz) shelled broad beans
2 carrots, sliced
½ green pepper, cored, deseeded and sliced
2 small onions, chopped
½ small cauliflower, broken into florets
salt and pepper
4 small tomatoes, skinned and chopped
SAUCE:
15 g (½ oz) butter
15 g (½ oz) plain flour
150 ml (¼ pint) milk
½ teaspoon made mustard
25 g (1 oz) Cheddar cheese, grated

Cream the potatoes with the butter and milk. Place the remaining vegetables, except the tomatoes, in a pan of boiling salted water. Return to the boil, cover and simmer for 15 to 20 minutes; drain.

Meanwhile, put the tomatoes in a small pan with salt and pepper to taste and simmer gently until pulped. Spoon the mixed vegetables into a dish and season well with salt and pepper. Spoon over the tomato pulp.

To make the sauce, melt the butter in a small pan, stir in the flour and cook for 1 minute. Gradually stir in the milk and cook for 2 to 3 minutes, stirring. Add salt and pepper to taste, the mustard and cheese. Spoon the sauce over the vegetables and cover with the potatoes.

Cook in a preheated moderately hot oven, 190°C (375°F), Gas Mark 5, for 20 minutes or until golden.

Serves 4

UNUSUAL VEGETARIAN CHEESES

Those cheeses that are clearly labelled 'vegetarian' are perhaps the first and best choice to buy for general use. There are however a number of unusual cheeses, some found in supermarkets, some found in health food shops, that are worth looking for. These include Botton, an English farmhouse cheese from Yorkshire that is made with chives; Coulommiers, a mild French cheese similar to Brie; Geska, a Swiss whey cheese; Chevre or French goat's cheese; Feta from Greece; and low fat Ricotta cheese made with whey not pressed curds.

Wholemeal Cheese Pudding

SULTANA AND NUT PILAFF

3 tablespoons sunflower oil
1 onion, sliced
2 sticks celery, sliced
250 g (8 oz) long-grain brown rice
600 ml (1 pint) vegetable stock
salt and pepper
175 g (6 oz) sultanas
125 g (4 oz) shelled pistachios
2 tablespoons chopped coriander
2 spring onions, sliced, to garnish

Heat the oil in a large pan and fry the onion and celery over moderate heat for 2-3 minutes, until they are beginning to soften. Add the rice and stir well. Pour on the stock, bring to the boil, cover and simmer over low heat for 35 minutes.

Season to taste with salt and pepper, add the sultanas and nuts and stir gently. Cover and simmer for a further 5-10 minutes, until the rice is just tender. Stir in the coriander, transfer to a warm serving dish and garnish with the spring onions.

Serves 4

FRUIT AND VEGETABLE KEBABS

1 large aubergine
2 courgettes
salt
125 g (4 oz) button mushrooms
3 small onions
175 g (6 oz) Ready-to-Eat dried apricots
2 bananas, thickly sliced
MARINADE:
3 tablespoons olive oil
2 tablespoons cider vinegar
1 tablespoon orange juice
salt and pepper

Cut the aubergine into 2.5 cm (1 inch) cubes and the courgettes into 2.5 cm (1 inch) slices. Place them in a colander, sprinkle with salt and leave to drain for 30 minutes. Rinse then drain.

Meanwhile, mix the marinade ingredients in a bowl, add the mushrooms, onions and apricots and leave for 30 minutes. Remove the ingredients with a draining spoon, reserving the marinade.

Thread the vegetables and fruit on to 4 skewers, brush them with the reserved marinade and cook under a preheated hot grill for 6-7 minutes, turning them once.

Serves 4

MIDDLE EASTERN RICE

50 g (2 oz) raisins
1 tablespoon boiling water
50 g (2 oz) butter
1 onion, chopped
250 g (8 oz) long-grain rice
450 ml (¾ pint) vegetable stock
salt and pepper
25 g (1 oz) pine kernels, toasted

Cover the raisins with the water and leave to soak.

Melt the butter in a flameproof casserole. Add the onion and fry for 5 minutes. Add the rice and stir for 2 to 3 minutes until well coated with the butter. Add the stock and salt and pepper to taste.

Transfer to a preheated moderate oven, 180°C (350°F), Gas Mark 4, for 35-40 minutes.

Add the pine kernels and raisins to the rice and mix lightly with a fork. Serve hot.

Serves 4

FALAFEL CROQUETTES

500 g (1 lb) chick peas, soaked for 24 hours
3 garlic cloves, crushed
2 teaspoons ground coriander
2 teaspoons ground cumin
2 tablespoons snipped chives
salt and pepper
oil for deep frying

Drain the chick peas thoroughly. Place in a blender or food processor with the garlic, coriander, cumin, chives and salt and pepper to taste. Process until well blended, adding a little water if necessary.

Divide and roll the chick pea mixture into about 40 small balls.

Shallow fry the falafel croquettes in hot oil, in batches, for about 2 to 3 minutes until golden. Drain on absorbent kitchen paper. Serve while still hot.

Serves 4 to 6

COUNTRY VEGETABLE FLAN

PASTRY:
50 g (2 oz) wholemeal flour
125 g (4 oz) plain flour, sifted
pinch of salt
75 g (3 oz) butter
2-3 tablespoons water
FILLING:
1 large carrot
1 leek
salt and pepper
25 g (1 oz) butter
25 g (1 oz) plain flour
300 ml (½ pint) milk
125 g (4 oz) grated Cheddar cheese
½ teaspoon mustard
50 g (2 oz) each broad beans, peas and sweetcorn, cooked

Prepare the pastry as for Spinach Cheese Flan (page 91). Roll out and use to line a 20 cm (8 inch) flan ring on a baking sheet. Bake blind in a preheated moderately hot oven, 190°C (375°F), Gas Mark 5, for 15 minutes. Remove the beans and foil and return to the oven for 5 minutes.

Meanwhile, make the filling. Slice the carrot and leek, then cook separately in boiling salted water until tender; drain. Melt the butter in a pan, stir in the flour and cook for 1 minute. Gradually blend in the milk, then heat, stirring, until thickened. Add 75 g (3 oz) cheese, the mustard, vegetables, and salt and pepper to taste.

Turn into the flan case and sprinkle with the remaining cheese. Place under a preheated moderate grill until the cheese is bubbling. Serve immediately.

Serves 4

GREEN BEAN AND LENTIL PIE

125 g (4 oz) red lentils
4 celery sticks
1 onion
125 g (4 oz) carrots
1 clove garlic
15 g (½ oz) butter
1 tablespoon oil
250 g (8 oz) frozen cut green beans
125 g (4 oz) frozen broad beans
1 × 283 g (10 oz) can extra thick vegetable soup
2 tablespoons chopped parsley
2 tablespoons chopped mint
125 g (4 oz) cheese, grated
salt and pepper
175 g (6 oz) shortcrust pastry (see Goat's Cheese Quiche page 81)
milk to glaze
parsley to garnish

Place the lentils in a bowl, cover with boiling water and leave to soak for 1 hour. Drain thoroughly. Slice the celery, onion and carrots. Chop the garlic.

Heat the butter and oil in a flameproof dish, add the celery and fry gently until softened; remove. Add the onion and carrots to the dish and sauté until softened. Return the celery to the dish, with the garlic, beans, lentils and soup. Bring to the boil and mix in the parsley, mint, cheese, and salt and pepper to taste. Simmer for 5 minutes.

Roll out the pastry to a circle large enough to cover the dish and decorate with leaves made from the trimmings. Brush with milk and bake in a preheated moderately hot oven, 200°C (400°F), Gas Mark 6, for 40 minutes. Serve hot, garnished with parsley.

Serves 4

Green Bean and Lentil Pie

VEGETABLE MEDLEY CASSEROLE

125 g (4 oz) aduki beans
125 g (4 oz) mung beans
salt and pepper
2 onions, sliced
1 × 397 g (14 oz) can chopped tomatoes
375 g (12 oz) tomatoes, sliced
2 cloves garlic, chopped
3 celery sticks, thinly sliced
125 g (4 oz) carrots, thinly sliced
2 bouquet garnis
2 tablespoons tomato and chilli relish
450 ml (¾ pint) vegetable stock
375 (12 oz) frozen cauliflower, thawed
15 g (½ oz) butter, melted
2 water biscuits, crumbled
50 g (2 oz) Cheddar cheese, grated
parsley to garnish

Soak the beans separately in cold water to cover overnight. Drain and rinse. Boil the beans separately in salted water for 10 minutes.

Put the aduki beans in a large flameproof casserole. Cover with half the onions and tomatoes, and the garlic. Place the mung beans on top and cover with the remaining onion, then the celery and carrot, and the remaining chopped tomatoes. Cover with the remaining tomatoes.

Tuck the bouquet garnis down the sides. Stir the relish into the stock and pour into the casserole. Bring to the boil, cover and cook in a preheated moderate oven, 180°C (350°F), Gas Mark 4, for 1 hour.

Add salt and pepper to taste and cook, uncovered, for 30 minutes. Discard the bouquet garnis.

Toss the cauliflower in the butter. Place on top of the casserole. Mix the biscuits and cheese together and sprinkle over the top.

Increase the oven temperature to 220°C (425°F), Gas Mark 7, and cook for 15 minutes, until golden brown. Garnish with parsley.

Serves 6

Vegetable Medley Casserole

BAKING BLIND

Flans, tarts and quiches are often baked 'blind' so that their bases do not become soggy or remain undercooked at the end of the final cooking time. To bake 'blind' cut a square of cooking foil or greaseproof paper slightly larger than the flan tin or dish and use it to line the base and sides. Weigh down with beans, pasta or rice if greaseproof paper is used. Cook for the time stated in the recipe then remove the beans, pasta or rice and foil or paper and return to the oven or cook as directed.

KITCHEN GARDEN HOTPOT

1 onion
250 g (8 oz) carrots
1 small cauliflower
4 tomatoes
1 tablespoon oil
300 ml (½ pint) vegetable stock
1 tablespoon tomato purée
1 teaspoon dried mixed herbs
salt and pepper
125 g (4 oz) frozen sweetcorn
1 courgette, sliced
DUMPLINGS:
50 g (2 oz) self-raising flour
25 g (1 oz) vegetable suet
1 tablespoon chopped parsley
75 g (3 oz) grated Cheddar cheese

Slice the onions and carrots. Break the cauliflower into florets. Skin and chop the tomatoes.

Heat the oil in a large pan, add the onion and carrots and fry for 5 minutes. Add the tomatoes, stock, tomato purée, herbs, and salt and pepper to taste. Bring to the boil, cover and simmer for 15 minutes. Add the cauliflower, sweetcorn and courgette and cook for 15 minutes.

Meanwhile, make the dumplings. Sift the flour into a bowl and add the suet, parsley, 50 g (2 oz) of the cheese, and salt and pepper to taste. Stir in 4 tablespoons water and mix to an elastic dough. Turn onto a floured surface and, with floured hands, shape into 8 balls.

Place the dumplings on top of the vegetables. Sprinkle with the remaining cheese, cover and simmer for 30 minutes.

Transfer to a warmed serving dish and serve immediately.

Serves 4

ABOVE: *Onion and Cream Tart*

ONION AND CREAM TART

PASTRY:
125 g (4 oz) plain flour
½ teaspoon salt
50 g (2 oz) butter
1 egg, beaten
1-2 teaspoons iced water
FILLING:
50 g (2 oz) butter
750 g (1½ lb) onions, sliced
3 egg yolks
250 ml (8 fl oz) double cream
salt and pepper
grated nutmeg

Sift the flour and salt together into a bowl. Rub in the butter until the mixture resembles fine breadcrumbs Mix in the egg and sufficient water to make a pliable dough. Wrap in foil and chill for 1 to 2 hours.

Melt the butter in a pan, add the onions and fry gently for about 30 minutes until golden brown. Cool. Beat the egg yolks and cream together, adding salt, pepper and nutmeg to taste. Add the onions and mix well.

Roll out the pastry very thinly and use to line a 20 cm (8 inch) flan tin. Fill with the onion mixture. Bake in a preheated moderately hot oven, 200°C (400°F), Gas Mark 6, for 30 to 40 minutes. Serve hot.

Serves 4 to 6

MUSHROOM QUICHE

175 g (6 oz) shortcrust pastry (see Goat's Cheese Quiche opposite)
50 g (2 oz) butter
500 g (1 lb) mushrooms, sliced
1 large onion, chopped
squeeze of lemon juice
salt and pepper
1 tablespoon plain flour
142 ml (¼ pint) carton double cream
1 egg, beaten

Roll out the pastry and use to line a 23 cm (9 inch) flan dish. Prick well with a fork. Line with greaseproof paper and beans. Bake blind in a preheated hot oven, 230°C (450°F), Gas Mark 8, for 10 minutes. Remove the beans and paper. Cool.

Melt the butter in a saucepan, and cook and mushrooms and onion gently until soft. Add the lemon juice and salt and pepper to taste. Sprinkle in the flour and cook, stirring, for 2 minutes. Cool. Beat the cream into the egg, then stir into the filling. Pour into the flan case.

Bake in a preheated moderately hot oven, 200°C (400°F), Gas Mark 6, for 20 to 25 minutes until set.

Serves 6

VEGETABLE QUICHE

175 g (6 oz) wholemeal pastry (see Spinach Cheese Flan page 91)
2 carrots, sliced
½ small cauliflower, cut into florets
25 g (1 oz) butter
25 g (1 oz) plain flour
250 ml (8 fl oz) milk
1 × 326 g (11 oz) can sweetcorn
2 eggs, beaten
2 tablespoons chopped parsley
2 tablespoons grated Cheddar cheese
salt and pepper

Roll out the pastry and use to line a 20 cm (8 inch) flan tin. Prick the base and bake blind in a preheated oven, 200°C (400°F), Gas Mark 6, for 15 minutes.

Cook the carrots and cauliflower in boiling salted water for 4 minutes. Drain.

Place the butter, flour and milk in a pan. Bring to the boil, whisking constantly, until smooth and thickened. Remove from the heat, add the drained sweetcorn, eggs and parsley, mixing well. Fold in the carrots and cauliflower with salt and pepper to taste. Spoon into the par-cooked pastry case and sprinkle with the cheese.

Return to the oven and cook for a further 25 to 30 minutes. Serve hot.

Serves 4 to 6

RIGHT: *Goat's Cheese Quiche; Gougère*

GOAT'S CHEESE QUICHE

PASTRY:
175 g (6 oz) plain flour
½ teaspoon salt
75 g (3 oz) butter
2-4 tablespoons iced water

FILLING:
25 g (1 oz) butter
75 g (3 oz) hard goat's cheese
50 g (2 oz) Ricotta or soft goat's cheese
175 g (6 oz) cream cheese
3 tablespoons double cream
2 eggs, beaten
1 tablespoon chopped chives
salt and pepper

Sift the flour and salt into a bowl and rub in the butter until the mixture resembles fine breadcrumbs. Mix in sufficient water to give a soft dough. Form into a ball; do not knead or chill. Lightly press into the base and sides of a 20 cm (8 inch) flan tin. Prick the base with a fork. Bake blind in a preheated moderately hot oven, 200°C (400°F), Gas Mark 6, for 20 minutes.

Meanwhile make the filling. Beat the butter until soft, then beat in the cheeses. Add the cream, eggs, chives, and salt and pepper to taste. Mix well and spoon into the prepared case. Return to the moderately hot oven and cook for 20 to 25 minutes, until golden brown and risen. Serve immediately.

Serves 4 to 6

GOUGÈRE

300 ml (½ pint) milk
50 g (2 oz) butter
1 teaspoon salt
150 g (5 oz) plain flour
4 eggs
125 g (4 oz) Double Gloucester cheese, grated
milk to glaze

Place the milk, butter and salt in a pan. Bring to the boil, remove from the heat and beat in the flour

Allow to cool slightly, then add the eggs, one at a time, beating until a shiny smooth paste is formed. Stir in 75 g (3 oz) of the cheese.

Using a piping bag fitted with a 2.5 cm (1 inch) plain nozzle, pipe the mixture onto a greased baking sheet, to form an 18 cm (7 inch) ring. Carefully pipe the remaining mixture on top, making a deep-edged ring.

Sprinkle with the remaining cheese. Brush with milk and bake in a preheated moderately hot oven, 190°C (375°F), Gas Mark 5, for 40 to 45 minutes until well risen and golden. Serve hot or cold.

Serves 4 to 6

VEGETABLE PASTIES

SHORTCRUST PASTRY:
125 g (4 oz) plain flour
pinch of salt
50 g (2 oz) butter
1 tablespoon cold water
FILLING:
75 g (3 oz) mixed vegetables, cooked
1 tablespoon baked beans
50 g (2 oz) Cheddar cheese, diced
1 tablespoon chutney
1 egg yolk, beaten
salt and pepper
milk to glaze
parsley sprigs to garnish

Make the pastry as for Spinach Cheese Flan (see page 91). Divide in half and roll each piece to a 15 cm (6 inch) circle.

Mix together the vegetables, beans, cheese, chutney, most of the egg yolk and salt and pepper to taste. Divide between the pastry circles, leaving a 1 cm (½ inch) border at the edges.

Add a little milk to the remaining egg yolk and use to brush the pastry edges. Fold the pastry in half, enclosing the filling, and press the edges together. Place on a baking sheet.

Make slits in the top and brush the pasties with the remaining egg and milk. Cook in a preheated moderately hot oven, 190°C (375°F), Gas Mark 5, for 20 to 25 minutes.

Serve hot or cold, garnished with parsley.

Serves 2

CHEDDAR EGG LOG WITH SALAD

4 hard-boiled eggs, chopped
250 g (8 oz) matured Cheddar cheese, grated
1 clove garlic, crushed
2 tablespoons mayonnaise
2 tablespoons double cream
1 tablespoon chopped parsley
salt and pepper
SALAD:
1 lettuce
½ cucumber, sliced
½ green pepper, cored, deseeded and sliced
4 tomatoes, sliced

Place the eggs, cheese, garlic, mayonnaise, cream and chopped parsley in a bowl. Mix well and add salt and pepper to taste.

With wet hands, shape the mixture into a roll. Wrap in foil and chill in the refrigerator for at least 1 hour.

Arrange the salad ingredients at the ends of an oval serving plate. Slice the log into 8 pieces and arrange along the middle of the plate. Serve with rolls and butter.

Serves 4

Vegetable Pasties; Cottage Cheese and Spinach Flan

COTTAGE CHEESE AND SPINACH FLAN

SHORTCRUST PASTRY:
75 g (3 oz) plain flour
pinch of salt
40 g (1½ oz) butter
1 tablespoon cold water
FILLING:
125 g (4 oz) frozen chopped spinach, thawed
salt and pepper
113 g (4 oz) cottage cheese, sieved
1 egg, beaten
2 tablespoons soured cream
grated nutmeg
25 g (1 oz) Cheddar cheese, grated

Make the pastry as for Spinach Cheese Flan (see page 91). Roll out and use to line a 15 cm (6 inch) flan dish or tin, standing on a baking sheet.

Drain the spinach thoroughly and place in the pastry case. Sprinkle with salt and pepper.

Mix together the cottage cheese, egg, soured cream and salt, pepper and nutmeg to taste. Pour over the spinach and sprinkle with the grated cheese.

Cook in a preheated moderately hot oven, 200°C (400°F), Gas Mark 6, for 25 to 35 minutes or until the filling is set. Serve hot or cold.

Serves 2 to 3

HARICOT HOT POT

250 g (8 oz) dried haricot beans, soaked
3 tablespoons sunflower oil
2 onions, sliced
4 celery sticks, sliced
2 carrots, diced
2 parsnips, diced
450 ml (¾ pint) vegetable stock
1 teaspoon yeast extract
salt and pepper
2 tablespoons chopped parsley
125 g (4 oz) button mushrooms, sliced

Drain the beans and place them in a saucepan with water to cover. Boil steadily for 10 minutes, lower the heat, cover and simmer for 40 minutes, until tender. Drain, rinse under cold water, then drain.

Heat the oil in a flameproof casserole and fry the onion and celery over moderate heat for 4-5 minutes. Add the carrots, parsnips, stock, yeast extract and beans and season to taste with salt and pepper. Cover the casserole, bring to the boil, then transfer to a preheated oven at 180°C, (350°F), Gas Mark 4, for 1¼ hours. Stir in the parsley and mushrooms and cook for 15 minutes.

Serves 4

CHEESY BEAN BAKE

125 g (4 oz) mixed dried beans (haricot, kidney and black-eye, for example)
15 g (½ oz) butter
1 small onion, chopped
1 carrot, sliced
1 celery stick, chopped
1 clove garlic, crushed
1 × 227 g (8 oz) can tomatoes
1 teaspoon dried marjoram
salt and pepper
75 g (3 oz) Cheddar cheese, grated

Place the beans in a bowl and cover with cold water. Place the kidney beans, if using, in a separate bowl and cover with water. Leave to soak overnight.

Drain and place the beans in a saucepan; put the kidney beans, if using, in a separate pan (to avoid tinting the others pink). Cover the pulses with fresh cold water. Bring to the boil and boil steadily for 10 minutes. Lower the heat, cover and simmer for 40 minutes or until tender. Drain, rinse under cold water, then drain.

Melt the butter in a saucepan, add the onion, carrot and celery and fry until soft. Stir in the garlic, pulses, tomatoes with their juice, marjoram and salt and pepper to taste.

Bring to the boil, cover and simmer for 1 to 1¼ hours, adding a little water if the mixture becomes dry. Check the seasoning. Transfer to a warmed serving dish. Sprinkle with the cheese. Serve immediately.

Serves 2

LENTILS AND BEANS – TO SOAK OR NOT TO SOAK

Lentils and split peas generally do not require soaking before cooking but almost all whole peas and beans do. Always follow the packet instructions or specific recipe instructions. There are, however, two basic methods for soaking – slow and quick. Pulses which have been soaked for a number of hours take less time to cook than if quick-soaked

QUICK SOAK: Place the washed pulses in a large pan, add at least 3 cups of cold water to each cup of pulse and bring to the boil. Boil for 2 minutes, remove from the heat, cover and leave for 1-2 hours until plump.

SLOW SOAK: Place the washed pulses in a bowl and add at least 3 cups of cold water to each cup of pulse. Soak in a cool place for several hours.

AUBERGINE BEAN BAKE

2 tablespoons oil
250 g (8 oz) aubergine
1 × 447 g (15 oz) can baked beans
1 tablespoon hot pepper sauce
227 g (8 oz) frozen sliced green beans
1 × 425 g (15 oz) can butter beans
250 g (8 oz) tomatoes sliced
¼ teaspoon dried thyme
2 tablespoons chopped parsley
salt and pepper
50 g (2 oz) Cheddar cheese

Heat the oil in a 1.5 litre (2½ pint) flameproof casserole. Cut the aubergine into 1 cm (½ inch) cubes and fry for 6 to 8 minutes; remove.

Pour the baked beans and pepper sauce into the casserole, off the heat. Cover with the green beans, then the drained butter beans and spread the aubergine evenly on top. Arrange the tomato in circles from the centre, leaving a border. Sprinkle with the thyme, parsley, and salt and pepper to taste.

Slice the cheese very thinly, then cut into triangles. Arrange on top, overlapping the tomato.

Cook in a preheated moderately hot oven, 200°C (400°F), Gas Mark 6, for 30 minutes. Serve hot.

Serves 4

WATERCRESS PLAIT

25 g (1 oz) butter
3 spring onions, sliced
175 g (6 oz) watercress, chopped
1 teaspoon lemon juice
salt and pepper
2 tablespoons oil
250 g (8 oz) button mushrooms, sliced
1 clove garlic crushed
25 g (1 oz) pine kernels
375 g (12 oz) wholemeal pastry (see Spinach Cheese Flan page 91)
beaten egg to glaze
1 tablespoon sesame seeds

Melt the butter in a pan, add the spring onions and fry over a moderate heat for 3-4 minutes, until soft. Add the watercress, lemon juice and salt and pepper to taste and cook for 5-6 minutes, stirring frequently. Turn onto a plate to cool.

Heat the oil and fry the mushrooms, garlic and pine kernels for 2-3 minutes. Season with salt and pepper and leave to cool.

Roll the dough on a floured surface to 30 × 36 cm (12 × 14 inches). Mark into 3 sections lengthways. Dampen the edges. Make diagonal slits along the outer sections 2.5 cm (1 inch) apart and 8 cm (3 inches) long.

Spread half the watercress mixture over the centre section, cover with the mushroom mixture, then the remaining watercress. Fold the pastry strips over the filling to give a plaited effect. Press the ends firmly to seal.

Lift onto a baking sheet, brush with egg and sprinkle with sesame seeds. Bake in a preheated oven at 200°C, 400 °F, Gas Mark 6 for 30 to 35 minutes, until golden brown. Serve with a salad.

Serves 4 to 6

LEFT: *Aubergine Bean Bake*

RIGHT: *Hearty Pumpkin Soup; Braised Leeks*

HEARTY PUMPKIN SOUP

750 g (1½ lb) pumpkin, diced
1 onion, chopped
50 g (2 oz) long-grain brown rice
500 g (1 lb) carrots, sliced lengthways
1 2 litres (2 pints) boiling vegetable stock
¼ teaspoon ground nutmeg
10 cm (4 inch) stick cinnamon, halved
¼ teaspoon ground mixed spice
salt and pepper
125 g (4 oz) frozen peas
1 orange to garnish

Place the pumpkin, onion, rice, carrots and boiling stock in a large pan. Add the spices, and salt and pepper to taste and simmer for about 45 minutes, until the rice is soft. Add the peas and cook for 5 minutes. Discard the cinnamon stick.

Cut 4 thin slices from the centre of the orange for garnish. Grate the rest of the rind and squeeze out the juice. Stir the grated rind and juice into the soup. Serve in individual soup bowls, garnished with a twisted orange slice.

Serve with wholewheat bread and parsley butter.

Serves 4

BRAISED LEEKS

500 g (1 lb) baby leeks
1 dessert apple, peeled, cored and cut into 8 pieces
1 × 432 g (15 oz) can red kidney beans, drained
1 clove garlic, crushed
SAUCE:
65 g (2½ oz) tomato purée
2 tablespoons oil
½ teaspoon ground coriander
150 ml (¼ pint) hot water
2 tablespoons white wine or stock
salt and pepper
TO GARNISH:
coriander or parsley leaves

Put the leeks in a large flameproof casserole. Add the apple, beans and garlic.

Mix the sauce ingredients together, seasoning with salt and pepper to taste, and pour into the casserole. Cover and cook gently for 20 to 25 minutes, until the leeks are just tender.

Garnish with coriander or parsley and serve hot.

Serves 4

CHICORY WITH LEMON SAUCE

750 g (1½ lb) chicory
salt and pepper
15 g (½ oz) butter
grated rind and juice of 1 small lemon
pinch of grated nutmeg
150 ml (¼ pint) vegetable stock
2 teaspoons cornflour
1 tablespoon cold water
chopped parsley to garnish

Blanch the chicory heads in boiling salted water for 3 minutes, then drain. Arrange in a shallow, ovenproof dish and dot with the butter.

Mix together the lemon rind and juice, nutmeg and stock. Season to taste with salt and pepper, then pour over the chicory. Cover with foil and cook in a preheated moderate oven, 160°C (325°F), Gas Mark 3, for 1 hour. Drain off the juices into a small pan. Keep the chicory hot.

Blend the cornflour with the water and stir into the juices. Heat gently, stirring until the sauce thickens, then cook for 1 to 2 minutes. Adjust the seasoning and pour over the chicory. Serve hot, garnished with parsley.
Serves 4

BAKED AUGERGINES

2 aubergines
2 teaspoons salt
15 g (½ oz) butter
1 onion, chopped
1 clove garlic, crushed
150 ml (¼ pint) vegetable stock
3 tomatoes, skinned and chopped
1 tablespoon chopped chives
1 tablespoon sweetcorn
salt and pepper
25 g (1 oz) breadcrumbs
25 g (1 oz) Edam cheese, grated

Cut the aubergines in half lengthways, slash the flesh and sprinkle with the salt. Place, cut side down, on a plate and leave for 1 hour. Rinse and drain, then remove and chop the flesh, reserving the skins.

Heat the butter in a pan, add the onion and fry until soft. Add the aubergine flesh, garlic, 2 tablespoons stock, tomatoes, chives, sweetcorn, salt and pepper to taste; cook until soft. Pile into the aubergine cases.

Place the aubergines in a shallow ovenproof dish. Mix together the breadcrumbs and cheese and sprinkle over the aubergines. Add the remaining stock to the dish, then cover with foil. Place in a preheated moderately hot oven, 190°C (375°F), Gas Mark 5, for 30 minutes.
Serves 4

COUNTRY PANCAKES

PANCAKES:
125 g (4 oz) plain flour
pinch of salt
1 egg
300 ml (½ pint) milk
15 g (½ oz) butter for frying
FILLING:
125 g (4 oz) mushrooms, chopped
1 onion, sliced
6 tomatoes, skinned and chopped
125 g (4 oz) green beans
1 teaspoon mixed herbs
salt and pepper
TO FINISH:
100 g (4 oz) Double Gloucester cheese, grated
parsley sprigs to garnish

Sift the flour and salt into a bowl. Make a well in the centre and add the egg and half the milk. Beat until smooth, then stir in the remaining milk.

Place the filling ingredients, with salt and pepper to taste, in a pan. Bring to the boil, cover and simmer for 10 minutes.

To make the pancakes, lightly grease an 18 cm (7 inch) non-stick frying pan with butter and place over a moderate heat. Pour in enough batter to cover the base. Cook until the underside is lightly browned, then toss or turn the pancake and cook the other side.

Repeat with the remaining batter to make 8 pancakes; stack them on a plate, with a piece of greaseproof paper between each one, over a pan of simmering water to keep hot.

Divide the filling between the pancakes, top with two-thirds of the cheese and fold up. Arrange in an ovenproof dish and sprinkle with the remaining cheese. Place under a preheated hot grill until the cheese is bubbling and golden. Serve immediately, garnished with parsley.
Serves 4

LEFT: *Chicory with Lemon Sauce; Baked Aubergines*

RIGHT: *Fruit and Cheese Platter*

FRUIT AND CHEESE PLATTER

1 lettuce
375 g (12 oz) cottage cheese
50 g (2 oz) Edam cheese, grated
2 tomatoes, diced
salt and pepper
4 large fresh peaches, stones removed and cut into quarters
250 g (8 oz) grapes, halved and deseeded

Arrange the lettuce on a large serving platter. Mix together the cottage cheese, Edam cheese and tomatoes. Season with salt and pepper to taste. Mix well and pile into the centre of the lettuce.

Arrange the peaches and grapes around the cheese and serve at once.
Serves 4

PASTA COLESLAW

500 g (1 lb) dried conchiglie
1/4-1/2 small red cabbage, shredded
1 onion, sliced
1/4 cucumber, diced
2 celery sticks, chopped
2 green dessert apples, cored and sliced
juice of 1 lemon
1 bunch of watercress
oil for shallow-frying
4 cloves garlic
2 slices stale bread, cubed

DRESSING:
150 g (5 oz) carton natural yogurt
1-2 cloves garlic, crushed
2 tablespoons each chopped parsley and chives
pinch of chilli powder

Cook the pasta according to the packet instructions. Drain and cool quickly under cold running water. Drain thoroughly and place in a large bowl. Stir in the cabbage, onion, cucumber and celery.

Toss the apple slices in the lemon juice and add to the bowl with the watercress.

Mix the dressing ingredients together and fold into the salad. Transfer to a serving dish.

Heat the oil in a pan, add the garlic cloves and fry until brown; discard. Add the bread cubes and fry until golden. Drain on kitchen paper and sprinkle over the salad. Serve immediately.

Serves 4 to 8

CHEESE, SPINACH AND MUSHROOM CRÊPE LAYER

BATTER:
250 g (8 oz) plain flour, sifted
300 ml (1/2 pint) milk
150 ml (1/4 pint) water
4 eggs
1/2 teaspoon salt
50 g (2 oz) butter, melted

FILLING:
25 g (1 oz) butter
2 shallots, chopped
250 g (8 oz) spinach, blanched for 2 minutes, drained and chopped
salt and pepper
450 ml (3/4 pint) cheese sauce (see Cheese and Vegetable Gratin page 93, though use the full amount of cheese – 125 g (4 oz)
125 g (4 oz) button mushrooms, sliced
1 clove garlic, crushed
113 g (4 oz) carton cottage cheese
1 egg, beaten

To make the batter, put the flour in a bowl and gradually beat in the remaining ingredients. Continue beating until smooth. Cover and chill for 2 hours.

Lightly oil a 17-18 cm (6½-7 inch) frying pan and place over moderate heat. Pour in just enough batter to cover the base of the pan. Cook until the underside is golden, then turn and cook the other side. Repeat with the remaining batter, stacking the cooked crêpes interleaved with greaseproof paper; keep warm.

To make the filling, melt half the butter in a pan, add the shallots and fry until soft. Stir in the spinach, and salt and pepper to taste; cook for 5 minutes. Stir in 3 tablespoons of the cheese sauce.

Melt the remaining butter in a small pan, add the mushrooms and garlic and fry gently until softened. Allow to cool, then stir into the cottage cheese. Add the egg with 3 tablespoons of the sauce; mix well.

Place a crêpe in a greased ovenproof dish and spread with some of the spinach mixture. Top with a crêpe and cover with some of the mushroom mixture. Repeat the layers until all the ingredients are used, finishing with a crêpe.

Spoon over the remaining cheese sauce. Cover with foil and bake in a preheated moderate oven, 180°C (350°F), Gas Mark 4, for 25 to 30 minutes. Cut into wedges and serve immediately.

Serves 4 to 6

LEFT: *Pasta Coleslaw*

RIGHT: *Greek Salad*

GREEK SALAD

1 kg (2 lb) tomatoes
2 each red and yellow peppers, cored
1½ cucumbers, diced
3 onions, sliced
250 g (8 oz) black olives
375 g (12 oz) Feta cheese, diced
2 tablespoons chopped parsley
DRESSING:
3 × 150 g (5 oz) cartons natural yogurt
2 teaspoons Dijon mustard
5 tablespoons lemon juice
2 tablespoons finely grated lemon rind
3 cloves garlic, crushed
small bunch chopped mint
salt and pepper

First make the dressing: put the yogurt, mustard, lemon juice and rind into a bowl and mix well. Stir in the garlic, mint, and salt and pepper to taste.

Thinly slice the tomatoes and peppers and arrange on a serving plate with the remaining salad ingredients. Spoon over the dressing and toss lightly to serve.

Serves 15

SWEETCORN TAGLIATELLE

250 g (8 oz) egg tagliatelle
salt and pepper
15 g (½ oz) butter
1 tablespoon oil
1 onion, sliced
1 × 326 g (11 oz) can sweetcorn
1 × 19 g (½ oz) packet white sauce mix
300 ml (½ pint) milk
1 teaspoon coarse grain mustard
TO GARNISH:
chopped parsley
chopped hazelnuts

Cook the tagliatelle in boiling, salted water for 8 minutes. Drain thoroughly and transfer to a warmed serving dish; keep hot.

Melt the butter and oil in the pan, add the onion and fry gently for 2 to 3 minutes. Add the drained corn and salt and pepper to taste and heat through.

Make up the white sauce with the milk, as directed on the packet. Add the mustard and mix well.

When the corn mixture is hot, pour over the tagliatelle with three-quarters of the sauce and toss well. Top with the reserved sauce and garnish with parsley and nuts.

Serves 4

PEPPER QUICHE

CHEESE PASTRY:
75 g (6 oz) wholemeal flour
½ teaspoon mustard
pinch of salt
pinch of chilli powder
75 g (3 oz) butter
75 g (3 oz) Cheddar cheese, grated
2-3 tablespoons water
FILLING:
2 tablespoons oil
1 onion, chopped
1 clove garlic, crushed
1 green and 1 red pepper, cored, deseeded and sliced
2 eggs
150 ml (¼ pint) milk
50 g (2 oz) breadcrumbs

Place the flour, mustard, salt and chilli powder in a mixing bowl. Rub in the butter until the mixture resembles breadcrumbs. Stir in the cheese, add the water and mix to a firm dough. Turn onto a floured surface and knead lightly until smooth. Roll out thinly and use to line a 23 cm (9 inch) flan ring placed on a baking sheet. Chill for 15 minutes.

Meanwhile, heat the oil in a pan, add the onion and fry until softened. Add the garlic and peppers and cook for 10 minutes. Mix the eggs and milk together, then stir in the pepper mixture, breadcrumbs, and salt and pepper to taste.

Pour into the flan case and bake in a preheated moderately hot oven, 190°C (375°F), Gas Mark 5, for 35 to 40 minutes until golden.

Serves 4

VEGETABLE MOUSSAKA

250 g (8 oz) courgettes
250 g (8 oz) aubergines, cubed
salt and pepper
¼ teaspoon ground oregano
375 g (12 oz) potatoes
1 large onion, sliced
SAUCE:
2 tablespoons tomato purée
1 tablespoon olive oil
2 cloves garlic, crushed
grated rind and juice of ½ lemon
300 ml (½ pint) vegetable stock
TOPPING:
150 g (5 oz) carton natural yogurt
1 egg, beaten
50 g (2 oz) Cheddar cheese, grated
TO GARNISH:
parsley sprigs

Cut the courgettes in half crossways, then lengthways into sticks. Place the aubergine in a lightly greased 1.75 litre (3 pint) deep casserole and sprinkle lightly with salt and pepper. Cover with the courgettes and sprinkle with the oregano and a little salt and pepper. Thickly slice the potatoes and arrange half on top of the courgettes. Cover with the onion, then the remaining potatoes, seasoning each layer with salt and pepper to taste.

Mix the sauce ingredients together and pour into the casserole. Cover and cook in a preheated moderate oven, 180°C (350°F), Gas Mark 4, for 1 hour.

Mix the topping ingredients together, pour over the potatoes and return to the oven for 30 minutes, until golden brown. Garnish with parsley and serve with crusty rolls.
Serves 4

MUSHROOM LAYER LOAF

125 g (4 oz) button mushrooms, sliced
50 g (2 oz) butter
2 tablespoons chopped parsley
6 slices stale bread, crusts removed
375 g (12 oz) flat mushrooms, chopped
250 g (8 oz) fresh white breadcrumbs
1 egg, beaten
1 teaspoon yeast extract, dissolved in a little boiling water
salt and pepper
8 tomatoes
SAUCE:
75 g (3 oz) natural yogurt
75 ml (3 fl oz) soured cream
grated rind of ½ lemon
1 teaspoon paprika

Grease a 1 kg (2 lb) loaf tin and line with foil, leaving enough to cover the top later. Grease the foil.

Arrange half the sliced mushrooms down centre of tin. Mix the butter and parsley and spread on the bread.

Mix the chopped mushrooms, breadcrumbs, egg and yeast extract together with salt and pepper to taste.

Arrange half the bread slices, overlapping, buttered side down on the mushroom slices, and cover with half the chopped mushroom mixture, pressing well down. Cover with the remaining sliced mushrooms, then the remaining mushroom mixture. Finish with the remaining bread and bring the foil over the top.

Place in a roasting tin. Pour in boiling water to a depth of 1 cm (½ inch). Cook in a preheated moderately hot oven, 190°F (375°F), Gas Mark 5, for 30 minutes. Open the foil. Cut a cross on each tomato and place around the loaf in the roasting tin. Cook for 15 minutes. Mix together the sauce ingredients. Serve the loaf and tomatoes with the sauce, and a Watercress, Courgette and Tomato Salad (see page 62).
Serves 4

LEFT: *Vegetable Moussaka*

SPINACH CHEESE FLAN

WHOLEMEAL PASTRY:
175 g (6 oz) wholemeal flour
pinch of salt
75 g (3 oz) margarine
2-3 tablespoons water
FILLING:
500 g (1 lb) spinach
salt and pepper
227 g (8 oz) carton cottage cheese
2 eggs
50 g (2 oz) Double Gloucester cheese, grated
150 ml (¼ pint) milk
grated nutmeg

Place the flour and salt in a mixing bowl and rub in the butter until the mixture resembles breadcrumbs. Add the water and mix to a firm dough, then turn onto a floured surface and knead lightly until smooth. Roll out thinly and use to line a 20 cm (8 inch) flan ring placed on a baking sheet. Chill for 15 minutes.

Meanwhile, prepare the filling. Put the spinach in a large pan with just the water clinging to the leaves after washing and a pinch of salt. Cook gently for 5 minutes, turning twice. Drain thoroughly and chop finely. Place in a bowl with the remaining ingredients, seasoning with salt, pepper and nutmeg to taste. Mix thoroughly.

Pour into the flan case, smooth the top and bake in a preheated moderately hot oven, 190°C (375°F), Gas Mark 5, for 35 to 40 minutes. Serve hot or cold.

Serves 4

NUTTY LASAGNE

750 g (1½ lb) parsnips, diced
25 g (1 oz) butter
2 tablespoons chopped parsley
6 sheets of no pre-cook lasagne
340 g (12 oz) carton cottage cheese
500 g (1 lb) frozen chopped spinach, thawed and drained
¼ teaspoon nutmeg
50 g (2 oz) Cheddar cheese, thinly sliced
25 g (1 oz) walnuts, roughly chopped
1 large tomato, halved

Cook the parsnips in boiling salted water in a 1.75 litre (3 pint) shallow flameproof dish for 12 to 15 minutes or until tender. Drain and mash in the dish with half the butter and the parsley.

Cover with half the lasagne, then the cottage cheese, then the remaining lasagne. Cover with the spinach and season with the nutmeg, salt and pepper to taste. Arrange the cheese slices along 2 sides of the dish.

Cook in a preheated moderate oven, 180°C (350°F), Gas Mark 4, for 30 minutes. Sprinkle the walnuts down the centre and dot with the remaining butter. Arrange the tomato on either side of the walnuts

Serves 4

STORING FRESH GINGER

Fresh ginger has a soft brown skin and moist, fibrous flesh. A whole piece can weigh up to 375 g (12 oz). To store it, wrap it closely in foil and keep it in the refrigerator for up to 3 weeks. Alternatively, scrape off the skin, thinly slice or grate the flesh and pack it in small screw-top jars covered with dry sherry or olive oil. It will keep in the refrigerator for up to one year. The ginger-flavoured sherry or oil can later be used in salad dressings and sauces.

SPICED VEGETABLE PANCAKES

500 g (1 lb) potatoes
salt
2 tablespoons oil
1 onion, chopped
1 clove garlic, chopped
1 cm (½ inch) piece fresh root ginger, chopped
1 teaspoon turmeric
½ teaspoon ground coriander seeds
2 tomatoes, peeled and chopped
hard-boiled egg slices, to garnish
PANCAKES
125 g (4 oz) plain wholemeal flour
1 egg
1 egg yolk
300 ml (½ pint) milk
oil for shallow frying

Cook the potatoes in boiling, salted water until they are tender. Drain them, reserving 150 ml (¼ pint) of the liquid. Heat the oil in a pan and fry the onion, garlic and ginger over moderate heat for 3-4 minutes.

Dice the potatoes and add them to the pan with the turmeric, ground coriander, tomatoes and the reserved liquid. Simmer, uncovered, for 5 minutes. Set the pan aside and keep the filling warm.

Sift the flour into a bowl with a pinch of salt and tip in any bran in the sieve. Make a well in the centre and add the egg, egg yolk and half the milk. Beat until smooth, then stir in the remaining milk.

Lightly brush an 18 cm (7 inch) non-stick frying pan with oil and place over a moderate heat. Pour in enough batter to cover the base and cook until the underside is lightly browned. Toss or turn the pancake and cook the other side.

Repeat with the remaining batter to make 8 pancakes, keeping them hot.

Divide the filling between them and roll them up. Garnish with the egg slices and serve hot.

Serves 4

CURRIED EGGS

8 eggs
2 tablespoons oil
2 onions, chopped
2 cloves garlic, crushed
2.5 cm (1 inch) piece fresh root ginger, chopped, or ½ teaspoon ground ginger
½ teaspoon ground cinnamon
1 teaspoon paprika
1 teaspoon salt
1 tablespoon mild curry powder
2 tablespoons desiccated coconut
6 tablespoons pineapple juice
300 ml (½ pint) vegetable stock
300 g (10 oz) natural yogurt
1 tablespoon garam masala (optional)

Place the eggs in a saucepan and cover completely with water. Bring to the boil over moderate heat and boil gently for 5 minutes.

Meanwhile, heat the oil in a heavy-based pan. Add the onions, garlic and root ginger, if using, and fry quickly for 3 minutes, stirring. Add the ground ginger, if using, cinnamon, paprika, salt and curry powder. Cook gently for about 10 minutes, stirring occasionally.

Meanwhile, shell the eggs and add to the onion mixture with the coconut, pineapple juice, stock and yogurt. Heat slowly until simmering and simmer for 20 minutes. Stir in the garam masala, if using, and simmer for a further 2 to 3 minutes.

Serve hot with boiled rice and side dishes of onion and tomato salad, toasted coconut, thinly sliced cucumber in natural yogurt, sliced banana in lemon juice, and chutneys.
Serves 4

SWEET POTATO PATTIES

750 g (1½ lb) sweet potato, cut into 1 cm (½ inch) cubes
salt and pepper
1 tablespoon soft light brown sugar
1½ teaspoons ground cardamom
75 g (3 oz) cornflakes, crushed
4 tablespoons oil
450 ml (¾ pint) dry cider
2 celery sticks, finely sliced
50 g (2 oz) broccoli, broken into very small florets
2 teaspoons plain flour
15 g (½ oz) butter

Cook the sweet potato in boiling salted water for about 15 minutes, until soft. Drain well and mash with the sugar, cardamom, and salt and pepper to taste. Divide into 4 portions and form into balls.

Spread the cornflakes out on a board. Place the potato balls on the board and flatten into cakes 8-10 cm (3-4 inches) in diameter. Turn to coat the other side with cornflakes.

Heat the oil in a frying pan, add the potato cakes and fry for 3 to 4 minutes on each side until brown, turning carefully. Transfer to a warmed serving dish and keep hot.

Pour the cider into the pan, add the celery, broccoli, and salt and pepper to taste. Bring to the boil and boil rapidly for 4 to 5 minutes.

Work the flour into the butter and add to the pan in small pieces. Bring to the boil, stirring, until a sauce is formed. Pour over the patties. Serve with coleslaw.
Serves 4

SPAGHETTI CARROTESE

375 g (12 oz) dried spaghetti
3 tablespoons olive oil
6 carrots, very thinly sliced
250 g (8 oz) tomatoes, skinned and chopped
3 tablespoons chopped basil
salt and pepper
50 g (2 oz) grated Double Gloucester cheese to serve

Cook the spaghetti in boiling salted water, according to the packet instructions. Drain and keep warm.

Meanwhile, heat the oil in a large frying pan and fry the carrots over a high heat until just cooked, about 5 to 10 minutes. Add the chopped tomatoes, basil and salt and pepper to taste, mixing well.

Pour the carrot and tomato sauce over the spaghetti and toss well to combine. Serve immediately sprinkled with the cheese.
Serves 4

AUBERGINE GALETTE

2 large aubergines
salt and pepper
150 ml (¼ pint) olive oil
1 onion, chopped
1 clove garlic, crushed
500 g (1 lb) tomatoes, skinned and chopped
1 egg
250 g (8 oz) Ricotta or curd cheese
1 tablespoon sesame seeds, toasted, to serve

Slice the aubergines, sprinkle with salt and leave in a colander for 1 hour. Rinse well and dry on kitchen paper.

Heat 2 tablespoons oil in a pan, add the onion and fry until softened. Add the garlic and tomatoes and simmer, uncovered, for 5 to 7 minutes.

Mix the egg with the cheese, adding salt and pepper to taste.

Heat the remaining oil in a frying pan, add the aubergines and cook on both sides until golden. Drain on kitchen paper.

Arrange a layer of overlapping aubergine slices on the bottom and sides of an 18 cm (7 inch) springform cake tin. Cover with half the tomato mixture, then top with half the cheese mixture. Repeat the layers, finishing with aubergine. Cover with foil and bake in a preheated moderate oven, 180°C (350°F), Gas Mark 4, for 40 to 50 minutes.

Turn out onto a warmed serving dish and sprinkle with the sesame seeds. Cut into wedges and serve with crusty wholewheat bread.
Serves 4.

LEFT: *Curried Eggs*

RIGHT: *Aubergine Galette*

CHEESE AND VEGETABLE GRATIN

2 tablespoons oil
2 onions, sliced
1 clove garlic, crushed
375 g (12 oz) courgettes, sliced
1 tablespoon chopped parsley
salt and pepper
4 large tomatoes, skinned and sliced
25 g (1 oz) butter
25 g (1 oz) wholemeal flour
300 ml (½ pint) milk
125 g (4 oz) Cheddar cheese, grated
1 tablespoon wholemeal breadcrumbs

Heat the oil in a pan, add the onions and fry gently until softened. Add the garlic, courgettes, parsley and salt and pepper to taste, and cook for 5 minutes, stirring occasionally.

Put half the mixture in a 1.5 litre (2½ pint) pie dish and cover with the tomatoes. Top with remaining mixture.

Melt the butter in a saucepan, stir in the flour, remove from the heat and blend in the milk. Bring to the boil, stirring constantly, until the sauce thickens. Add half of the cheese, and salt and pepper and pour over the courgettes. Sprinkle with the breadcrumbs, then the remaining cheese. Bake in a preheated moderate oven, 180°C (350°F), Gas Mark 4, for 30 minutes, until golden.
Serves 4

NOODLES WITH NUTS

125 g (4 oz) mange tout
2 tablespoons oil
1 onion, sliced
1-2 cloves garlic, sliced
1-2 teaspoons ground coriander
2 dried red chillies
300 g (10 oz) dried vermicelli
4 spring onions
125 g (4 oz) mushrooms
1 tablespoon chopped coriander
50 g (2 oz) pine kernels
50 g (2 oz) flaked almonds, browned
DRESSING:
4 tablespoons olive oil
2 teaspoons soy sauce
1 teaspoon clear honey

Cook the mange tout in boiling water for 1 minute, drain and set aside.

Heat the oil in a pan, add the onion and cook until golden. Add the garlic and coriander, then crumble in the chillies. Fry over a low heat for 2 minutes, stirring constantly. Remove from the heat and set aside.

Cook the vermicelli according to the packet instructions. Drain and cool quickly under cold running water. Drain and place in a large bowl. Add the cooked spices and mix well.

Chop the spring onions and slice the mushrooms. Add to the vermicelli with the mange tout and coriander, and season to taste.

Mix the dressing ingredients together, pour over the salad and mix well. Transfer to a serving dish and sprinkle with the pine kernels and almonds. Garnish with lime slices and coriander.

Serves 4 to 6

RED PEPPER AND LENTIL CROQUETTES

2 tablespoons oil
1 onion, chopped
2 celery sticks, chopped
1 red pepper, deseeded and finely chopped
250 g (8 oz) lentils
600 ml (1 pint) water
1 teaspoon ground coriander
salt and pepper
2 tablespoons chopped parsley
175 g (6 oz) wholemeal breadcrumbs
2 tablespoons flour
1 egg, beaten
oil for shallow-frying
YOGURT SAUCE:
300 g (10 oz) carton natural yogurt
1 tablespoon chopped coriander
1 clove garlic, crushed
TO GARNISH:
coriander sprigs

Heat the oil in a pan, add the onion, celery and red pepper and fry until softened. Add the lentils, water, coriander, and salt and pepper to taste. Bring to the boil, cover and simmer for 50 minutes to 1 hour, stirring occasionally. Mix in the parsley and one third of the breadcrumbs. Turn onto a plate to cool.

Using floured hands, shape the mixture into rissoles and coat with the flour. Dip into the beaten egg and coat with the remaining breadcrumbs.

Pour the oil into a frying pan to a depth of 5 mm (¼ inch) and place over moderate heat. When hot, add the rissoles and fry until crisp and golden brown, turning once or twice.

To make the sauce, mix the yogurt, coriander and garlic together. Serve the rissoles garnished with coriander and accompanied by the sauce.

Serves 4

MUSHROOM SAUCE

2 tablespoons oil
1 onion, chopped
1 clove garlic, crushed
125 g (4 oz) mushrooms, chopped
1 tablespoon wholemeal flour
75 ml (3 fl oz) vegetable stock
75 ml (3 fl oz) milk
2 teaspoons soy sauce
salt and pepper

Heat the oil in a pan, add the onion and fry until softened. Add the garlic and mushrooms and cook for about 2 minutes. Stir in the flour, then remove from the heat and stir in the stock and milk. Bring to the boil, stirring, and cook for 3 minutes. Stir in the soy sauce, and season.

Cool slightly, then work in a blender or food processor until smooth. Reheat gently.

Serve with nut roasts and rissoles.

Makes 450 ml (¾ pint)

ABOVE: *Noodles with Nuts*
RIGHT: *Tomato and Pepper Sauce; Tomato Sauce; Piquant Sauce; Red Pepper and Lentil Croquettes*

TOMATO AND PEPPER SAUCE

4 tablespoons oil
4 onions, chopped
2 large green peppers, cored, deseeded and chopped
2 × 397 g (14 oz) cans chopped tomatoes
salt and pepper
½ teaspoon French mustard
1 bay leaf
1 tablespoon cornflour, blended with 2 tablespoons water

Heat the oil in a pan, add the onion and green pepper and fry until soft. Add the tomatoes with their juice, salt and pepper to taste, mustard and bay leaf. Simmer for about 30 minutes, until reduced to a thick pulp. If a thick sauce is required, stir in the blended cornflour and bring to the boil; simmer, stirring, until thickened.

Serve with pasta.

Makes about 1.2 litres (2 pints)

TOMATO SAUCE

2 tablespoons olive oil
1 onion, chopped
1 clove garlic, crushed
500 g (1 lb) tomatoes, skinned and chopped
150 ml (¼ pint) vegetable stock
2 teaspoons tomato purée
1 bay leaf
salt and pepper

Heat the oil in a pan, add the onion and fry for 5 minutes, until softened. Add the remaining ingredients, with salt and pepper to taste, cover and simmer for 20 minutes, stirring occasionally.

Cool slightly and remove the bay leaf. Work in a blender or food processor until smooth, or rub through a sieve. Reheat gently.

Makes 350 ml (12 fl oz)

PIQUANT SAUCE

150 g (5 oz) carton natural yogurt
1 teaspoon tomato purée
½ teaspoon cumin powder
1 teaspoon ground coriander
1 teaspoon clear honey

Place all the ingredients in a small bowl and mix together thoroughly.

Makes 150 ml (¼ pint)

SUPPERS AND SNACKS

If you thought that a vegetarian supper or snack meant the inevitable omelette then you will have some delightful surprises in store. In this chapter you will find a whole host of tasty snack and supper-style dishes that will suit the most discriminating of gourmets. There are savoury melt-in-the-mouth rarebits, scrambled and devilled egg concoctions, stuffed potatoes with savoury fillings, quick pizza ideas and sizzling fried sandwich selections. There are of course some omelette ideas but the ones here have culinary inspiration with continental-style fillings or are cooked with vegetables to make tasty and sliceable wedges – a far cry from the simple egg and cheese option.

Like many of the recipes in this book these selections can be used imaginatively to double up as hearty appetizers, make light lunch as well as supper meals, will provide ideas for some main course accompaniments and some, like Cheese and Orange Eclairs, will make ideal finger food for serving with drinks or at a buffet style meal occasion.

OMELETTES

There are basically two types of omelette, the traditional French plain omelette, which is usually savoury and served loosely rolled, and the soufflé omelette, which can be savoury but is often served as a dessert, folded or 'open faced'.

The Spanish omelette is a French plain omelette with a substantial savoury filling, served 'open faced' or in wedges.

The best omelette pans are heavy-based for even heat distribution and are often, though not necessarily, non-stick. A 2- to 3-egg mixture needs a 15 cm (6 inch) pan and will serve one person.

Preheat the pan over a moderate heat for 1 to 2 minutes, then add the butter. If the temperature is correct, the butter will melt and sizzle quickly but not brown; if it doesn't, heat until the butter sizzles. Add the eggs and cook until set. A French plain omelette should be cooked and served in about 60 seconds.

A soufflé or filled omelette will take longer; the exact time depends on the type and amount of filling.

SPINACH OMELETTE

40 g (1½ oz) butter
250 g (8 oz) spinach, finely chopped
1 tablespoon natural yogurt
grated nutmeg
salt and pepper
4 eggs

Melt 25 g (1 oz) of the butter in a pan. Add the spinach and cook over a gentle heat for 4 to 5 minutes, stirring occasionally. Remove from the heat and stir in the yogurt. Season with nutmeg, salt and pepper to taste and keep hot.

Beat the eggs in a bowl, with salt and pepper to taste. Melt the remaining butter in a 28 cm (10 inch) omelette pan. When the butter is foaming, pour in the eggs. When the omelette begins to set, lift the cooked edge to allow the unset egg to run onto the pan.

Place the filling in the centre of the omelette, cook for 1 minute then fold in half. Slide onto a warmed plate and serve immediately.

Serves 2

PLAIN OMELETTE

2 or 3 eggs
salt and pepper
15 g (½ oz) butter

Break the eggs into a bowl, add salt and pepper to taste and beat lightly with a fork until well mixed but not frothy. Melt the butter in a preheated pan until sizzling. Add the eggs immediately. As the edge begins to set, draw the mixture towards the centre with a fork and, at the same time, tilt the pan slightly allowing the uncooked egg to run from the centre onto the hot base of the pan to set quickly.

When the omelette is lightly browned underneath but still soft and creamy on top, tilt the pan and fold over about one third of the omelette towards the centre, using a fork or palette knife. Fold over again, making a very loose roll, and turn onto a warmed serving plate. Serve immediately.

Serves 1

ABOVE: *Spinach Omelette* RIGHT: *Herb Omelette*

HERB OMELETTE

6 large eggs, beaten
salt and pepper
2 tablespoons chopped mixed herbs (e.g. parsley, tarragon, chives, chervil)
50 g (2 oz) butter
TO GARNISH:
parsley sprigs
knob of butter

Season the eggs with salt and pepper, add half the herbs and stir well. Melt the butter in a large omelette pan. When sizzling, stir in the eggs. Lower the heat and tilt the pan, moving the cooked mixture towards the centre with the back of a fork.

When the omelette is set and browned underneath, sprinkle the remaining herbs over the surface, fold in half and slide onto a warmed serving dish.

Garnish with parsley and a knob of butter and serve immediately.

Serves 4

PASTA OMELETTE WEDGES

175 g (6 oz) dried small wholemeal pasta spirals
25 g (1 oz) butter
1 small onion, chopped
½ green pepper, cored, deseeded and chopped
6 eggs
1 clove garlic, crushed
2 tomatoes, skinned and chopped
75 g (3 oz) Cheddar cheese, cubed
1 tablespoon snipped chives
salt and pepper

Cook the pasta in boiling salted water, according to the packet instructions. Drain well.

Meanwhile, melt the butter in a large omelette pan, add the onion and green pepper and cook for 5 minutes until softened.

Beat the eggs with the garlic, then stir in the tomatoes, cheese, chives and salt and pepper to taste.

Add the egg mixture to the omelette pan and cook for 4 minutes, lifting the set edges of the omelette to allow the liquid egg mixture to cook, or until the eggs are half set. Gently fold in the pasta and cook for a further 2 minutes, or until the eggs are nearly set. Remove the pan from the heat and cook under a preheated hot grill for 2 minutes or until the top is golden.

Cut into wedges to serve.

Serves 4

PANCAKES OR CRÊPES

Pancakes and crêpes are made from a similar mixture, though crêpes are sometimes made with buckwheat flour (available in healthfood shops), while pancakes are usually made with plain or wholemeal flour. If using wholemeal flour, stir in a little more liquid before using. If a batter is made several hours before required it will thicken and should be thinned down with more liquid – water will do.

Fritter batter must be very thick in order to coat the food being cooked thoroughly, without running off. Less liquid is used and the egg white is separated and whisked with an extra white, then folded into the batter. Dipping the food in flour first also helps the batter to stick.

TO COOK PANCAKES OR CRÊPES

Very lightly grease an omelette pan or heavy-based frying pan and place over a high heat until really hot. The easiest way to grease the pan is to rub a block of fat very lightly over the surface of the pan between cooking each pancake or crêpe.

Pour in just enough batter to cover the base very thinly, tilting the pan to ensure it is evenly distributed. When the edges are tinged golden brown and bubbles appear on the surface, toss or turn with a palette knife and cook the other side until golden brown. The side that is cooked first will have a lacy golden brown pattern and should become the outside when the pancake or crêpe is rolled or folded.

Turn onto a warmed heatproof plate, cover and place in a preheated cool oven, 150°C (300°F), Gas Mark 2, or over a pan of hot water to keep hot while cooking the remaining batter.

BASIC BATTERS

The method for making these batters is the same (see below). The quantities given are sufficient to make 16 to 20 small pancakes – about 15 cm (6 inches) in diameter.

SWEET PANCAKE BATTER

125 g (4 oz) plain or wholemeal flour
pinch of salt
2 teaspoons caster sugar
1 egg
300 ml (½ pint) milk
25g (1 oz) butter, melted
Makes 475 ml (16 fl oz)

Sift the dry ingredients into a mixing bowl and make a well in the centre. Add the egg(s) and half the liquid. Gradually mix in the flour to make a smooth, thick batter. Stir in the remaining liquid, melted butter and any flavourings. Beat for 2 to 3 minutes. Pour into a jug and use as required.

If using a blender or food processor, place all ingredients, except half the flour, in the goblet and blend for 30 seconds. Add the remaining flour and blend for a further 30 seconds.

SWEET CRÊPE BATTER

125 g (4 oz) plain, wholemeal or buckwheat flour
pinch of salt
50 g (2 oz) caster sugar
2 eggs
250 ml (8 fl oz) milk
25 g (1 oz) butter, melted
½ teaspoon vanilla essence
Makes 500 ml (18 fl oz)

SAVOURY PANCAKE BATTER

Omit the sugar. Increase the salt to ¼ teaspoon.

SAVOURY CRÊPE BATTER

Omit the sugar and vanilla. Increase salt to ¼ teaspoon. Replace milk with pale ale.

SAVOURY PANCAKES WITH CHEESE

1 quantity Savoury Pancake Batter (see page 100)
FILLING:
250 g (8 oz) cream cheese with garlic and herbs
3 spring onions, chopped
25 g (1 oz) walnuts, chopped
salt and pepper
15 g (½ oz) butter, melted
2 tablespoons chopped parsley to garnish

Lightly grease a 20 cm (8 inch) omelette pan or heavy-based frying pan and heat until very hot.

Pour in enough batter to make a very thin pancake, tilting the pan to ensure an even thickness. When the edges begin to brown and bubbles appear on the surface, toss and cook on the other side until golden. Turn onto a warmed heatproof plate, cover and keep warm while cooking the remaining batter. Make 8 pancakes.

Meanwhile, beat the cheese until softened. Fold in the spring onions and walnuts with salt and pepper to taste. Spread a little over each pancake then roll or fold into quarters and place in a shallow ovenproof serving dish. Drizzle with the melted butter.

Bake in a preheated moderate oven, 180°C (350°F), Gas Mark 4, for 5 to 10 minutes until the pancakes and their filling are heated through but not totally melted. Garnish with chopped parsley.

Serves 4

NORMANDY PANCAKES

1 quantity Savoury Pancake Batter (see page 100)
FILLING:
375 g (12 oz) frozen leaf spinach
2 large tomatoes, skinned and chopped
142 ml (¼ pint) carton soured cream
pinch of grated nutmeg
300 ml (½ pint) cheese sauce (see page 22)
salt and pepper

Lightly grease a 20 cm (8 inch) omelette pan or heavy-based frying pan and heat until very hot.

Pour in enough batter to make a very thin pancake, tilting the pan to ensure an even thickness. When the edges begin to brown and bubbles appear on the surface, toss and cook on the other side until golden. Turn onto a warmed heatproof plate, cover and keep warm while cooking the remaining batter. Make 8 pancakes.

Meanwhile, cook the spinach according to the packet instructions and drain well. Place in a pan with the tomatoes and heat gently. Add all but 2 tablespoons of the soured cream, the nutmeg and salt and pepper to tasted. Stir the remaining soured cream into the hot cheese sauce.

To serve, place a spoonful of spinach mixture in the centre of each pancake, roll up and place on a serving plate. Top with the sauce and serve immediately.

Serves 4 to 6

ASPARAGUS AND CHEESE SOUFFLÉ OMELETTE

6 eggs, separated
salt and pepper
375 g (12 oz) frozen and thawed, or canned asparagus spears, drained
2 tablespoons water
125 g (4 oz) matured Cheddar cheese, grated
25 g (1 oz) butter

Put 3 egg yolks in a small bowl with salt and pepper to taste. Reserve a few asparagus spears for garnish; roughly chop the remainder. Stir 1 tablespoon of the water and half the cheese and asparagus into the egg yolks. Whisk the 3 whites until very stiff, then carefully fold into the egg yolk mixture.

Melt half the butter in a 20 cm (8 inch) omelette pan, pour in the egg mixture and spread evenly. Cook over a low heat for 5 minutes, until the underneath is golden brown. Place the pan under a preheated hot grill for 1 minute, until the omelette is lightly browned on top and puffy.

Repeat with the remaining ingredients to make another omelette. Garnish with the reserved asparagus and serve immediately, folded if liked, with garlic bread.
Serves 4

CREAMED MUSHROOMS ON TOAST

50 g (2 oz) butter
1 small onion, chopped
375 g (12 oz) small button mushrooms
2 tablespoons plain flour
300 ml (½ pint) milk
2 tablespoons single cream (optional)
salt and pepper
juice of ½ lemon
4 slices hot buttered toast
parsley sprigs to garnish

Melt the butter in a pan, add the onion and cook for 5 to 7 minutes, without browning, until tender. Stir in the mushrooms and cook for 1 minute, stirring well. Sprinkle over the flour and mix well. Gradually add the milk, stirring constantly. Bring to the boil, then simmer for 2 minutes. Add the cream, if using, and salt and pepper to taste. Remove from the heat and stir in the lemon juice.

Put the toast on 4 warmed individual plates and spoon the mushrooms on top. Garnish with parsley and serve immediately.
Serves 4

CHEESE SOUFFLÉ

50 g (2 oz) Double Gloucester cheese, grated
300 ml (½ pint) Béchamel Sauce (see Lettuce Soup, page 16)
4 large eggs, separated
pinch of chilli powder

Grease a 900 ml (1½ pint) soufflé dish. Add the cheese to the hot béchamel sauce and stir over low heat until melted. Remove from the heat, cool slightly, then stir in the egg yolks and chilli powder.

Whisk the egg whites until stiff. Carefully fold into the cheese mixture. Spoon into the soufflé dish.

Cook in a preheated moderately hot oven, 200°C (400°F), Gas Mark 6, for 25 minutes until well risen and golden brown. Serve immediately.
Serves 4

LEFT: *Asparagus and Cheese Soufflé Omelette; Creamed Mushrooms on Toast*

RIGHT: *Cheese and Orange Éclairs*

CHEESE AND ORANGE ÉCLAIRS

CHOUX PASTRY:
150 ml (¼ pint) water
50 g (2 oz) butter
65 g (2½ oz) plain flour, sifted
salt and pepper
2 eggs, beaten
50 g (2 oz) Cheddar cheese, grated
FILLING:
75 g (3 oz) medium fat curd cheese
75 g (3 oz) matured Cheddar cheese, finely grated
finely grated rind of 1 orange
1 × 312 g (10 oz) can satsuma oranges, drained and chopped
6 tablespoons double cream, whipped
TO GARNISH:
orange slices

Make the choux pastry as for Gougère (see page 81).

Spoon the mixture into a piping bag, fitted with a 1 cm (½ inch) plain nozzle, and pipe 5 cm (2 inch) lengths, or small mounds onto greased baking sheets, spacing them well apart.

Bake in a preheated moderately hot oven, 200°C (400°F), Gas Mark 6, for 20 minutes, or until well risen and golden brown. Make a slit in the side of each éclair to allow the steam to escape. Transfer to a wire rack to cool.

Meanwhile, make the filling. Place the curd cheese in a bowl and blend in the Cheddar, orange rind and satsuma oranges. Fold in the cream.

Fill the éclairs with the cheese mixture and arrange on a serving plate. Garnish with orange slices.

Makes 18

PANCAKE PARCELS

4 hard-boiled eggs, finely chopped
3-4 tablespoons salad cream
1-2 teaspoons curry powder
1 carton cress, chopped
salt
8 × 18 cm (7 inch) savoury pancakes (see page 87)
1 egg, well beaten
125 g (4 oz) fresh white breadcrumbs
oil for deep frying

Mix together the eggs, salad cream, curry powder, cress, and salt to taste. Spread a little of the mixture onto each pancake. Fold two edges in to meet in the centre, then roll up, completely enclosing the filling.

Brush with beaten egg and roll in the breadcrumbs, taking care to seal the opening. Place close together in a frying basket with the sealed opening underneath. Heat the oil to 180°-190°C (350°-375°F), or until a cube of bread browns in 30 seconds. Deep-fry in hot oil for 3 to 4 minutes, until crisp and golden. Drain and serve.

Serves 4

BAKED CHEESE AND MUSTARD PUDDING

4 thick slices brown or white bread, crusts removed
50 g (2 oz) butter
1-2 tablespoons English mustard
175 g (6 oz) Cheddar cheese, grated
pepper
2 eggs
2 egg yolks
150 ml (¼ pint) vegetable stock, cooled
tomato slices to garnish

Spread both sides of the bread thickly with the butter and mustard to taste.

Put 2 slices in a well buttered pie dish. Cover with half the cheese and sprinkle with a little pepper. Top with the remaining bread.

Beat together the eggs and egg yolks and stir in the stock. Pour over the bread and top with the remaining cheese.

Cook in a preheated moderately hot oven, 190°C (375°F), Gas Mark 5, for 25 to 30 minutes until golden.

Garnish with tomato slices and serve immediately.

Serves 4

MUMBLED EGGS

This is a nineteenth-century dish which was originally eaten in gentlemen's clubs. It would now be best served for supper or a leisurely breakfast.

50 g (2 oz) button mushrooms
8 eggs
2 teaspoons English mustard
salt and pepper
50 g (2 oz) butter
113 g (4 oz) carton cream cheese
2 tablespoons single cream
2 tablespoons chopped parsley (optional)

Chop the mushrooms in a food processor. Add the eggs, mustard, and salt and pepper to taste. Process for 5 seconds, or until the eggs are amalgamated.

Melt the butter in a pan, add the mushroom and egg mixture, and the cream cheese, and stir over a low heat until the eggs are set. Stir in the cream just before serving.

Sprinkle with parsley if preferred, and serve with buttered toast or warm rolls.

Serves 4

JACKET POTATOES

Cheap but delicious, these make an excellent accompaniment to a vegetarian main course or, with a tasty filling, an ideal snack on their own.

4 large potatoes
oil for brushing
butter to serve

Brush the potatoes all over with oil and cook in a preheated moderately hot oven, 200°C (400°F), Gas Mark 6, for about 1 hour or until soft.

Cut a large deep cross in one side, fill generously with butter and serve immediately, or use any of the following fillings.

Serves 4

MUSHROOM AND CHEESE FILLING:

25 g (1 oz) butter
1 small onion, chopped
125 g (4 oz) button mushrooms, sliced
2 tablespoons soured cream or natural yogurt
2 tablespoons chopped chives
50 g (2 oz) matured Cheddar cheese, grated
salt and pepper
chopped chives to garnish

Melt the butter in a small pan and fry the onion over moderate heat until softened. Add the mushrooms and fry for 3-4 minutes. Stir in the soured cream or yogurt, the chopped parsley and half the cheese.

Remove the baked potatoes from the oven, cut in half lengthways, scoop out the flesh and mash until smooth. Beat in the filling mixture and season to taste with salt and pepper. Spoon into the potato shells, sprinkle with the remaining cheese and bake as above.

Garnish with parsley and serve immediately.

Serves 4

BROCCOLI AND CREME FRAICHE FILLING:

250 g (8 oz) brocolli spears
salt
150 ml (1/4 pint) carton soured cream
2 tablespoons chopped almonds
grated nutmeg
pepper
watercress sprigs to garnish

Cook the broccoli in boiling salted water for 6-8 minutes, until is it just tender. Drain and chop it.

Remove the baked potatoes from the oven, cut in half lengthways, scoop out the flesh and mash until smooth. Beat in the broccoli, crème fraîche and almonds and season to taste with nutmeg, salt and pepper. Spoon the mixture back into the potato shells. Place on a baking sheet and return to the oven for 15 minutes.

Garnish with watercress and serve immediately.

Serves 4

LEFT: *Mumbled Eggs*

RIGHT: *Potatoes with Cheese*

TOMATO AND CHEESE SAVOURIES

4 pieces pitta bread
65 g (2½ oz) tomato purée
500 g (1 lb) tomatoes, thinly sliced
125 g (4 oz) mushrooms, thinly sliced
½-1 teaspoon garlic salt
½-1 teaspoon dried marjoram
½-1 teaspoon dried basil
salt and pepper
125 g (4 oz) Cheddar cheese, grated

Spread the bread thinly with tomato purée, then cover with tomato and mushroom slices. Sprinkle with the garlic salt, herbs and salt and pepper to taste. Top with the grated cheese.

Place on a greased baking sheet and bake in a preheated moderately hot oven, 200°C (400°F), Gas Mark 6, for 15 minutes, or until the cheese has melted and the bread is heated through.

Serves 4

ENGLISH CHEESE FONDUE

1 small clove garlic, halved
15 g (½ oz) butter
6 tablespoons dry cider
125 g (4 oz) mature Cheddar cheese, grated
125 g (4 oz) Double Gloucester cheese, crumbled
1 teaspoon cornflour
1 tablespoon brandy
pepper
grated nutmeg
cubes of crusty bread to serve

Rub the inside of a fondue dish, flameproof casserole or saucepan with the cut garlic clove. Add the butter and cider and heat gently. Add the cheeses and cook gently, stirring, until melted.

Blend the cornflour and brandy to a smooth paste. Add pepper and nutmeg to taste and stir into the fondue. Continue to cook for 3 to 4 minutes until smooth and creamy.

To serve: Keep the fondue warm at the table, preferably over a spirit burner. Place the bread on a serving plate. Each person then spears a piece of bread onto a long-handled fondue fork and dips it into the fondue. Serve accompanied by a green salad.

POTATOES WITH CHEESE

½ teaspoon garlic salt
750 g (1½ lb) potatoes, sliced
salt and pepper
grated nutmeg
250 g (8 oz) Cheddar cheese, grated
300 ml (½ pint) milk

Grease an ovenproof dish and sprinkle with garlic salt. Arrange a third of the potato in the dish and season to taste with salt, pepper and nutmeg. Cover with a third of the cheese. Repeat the layers until the potatoes and cheese have been used up, then pour the milk over the top.

Cook in a preheated moderate oven, 180°C (350°F), Gas Mark 4, for 1 hour or until tender. Serve with French bread.

Serves 6

CURRIED EGG SALAD

150 ml (¼ pint) mayonnaise
4 tablespoons double cream
1 tablespoon curry paste
salt and pepper
6 hard-boiled eggs, quartered
1 crisp lettuce
watercress to garnish

Mix together the mayonnaise, cream and curry paste. Season with salt and pepper to taste. Carefully fold in the eggs.

Line a serving dish with the lettuce. Pile the egg mixture in the centre and garnish with watercress.

Serves 4

CHEESY BAPS

15 g (½ oz) butter
125 g (4 oz) Double Gloucester cheese, grated
½ teaspoon French mustard
1 teaspoon milk
salt and pepper
2 baps
1 tomato, skinned and sliced
parsley sprigs to garnish

Melt the butter in a saucepan and add the cheese. Cook over a low heat, stirring, until the cheese has melted. Stir in the mustard, milk and salt and pepper to taste.

Slice the baps in half and toast the cut side. Spread with the cheese mixture and top with the tomato slices. Place under a preheated medium grill for 2 to 3 minutes. Garnish with parsley. Serve immediately.

Serves 2

ONION AND TOMATO SCRAMBLE

3 eggs
2 tablespoons single cream
salt and pepper
25 g (1 oz) butter
½ small onion, finely chopped
1 tomato, skinned and chopped
2 slices bread, toasted

Beat the eggs with the cream and salt and pepper to taste.

Melt half the butter in a small saucepan, add the onion and fry until soft. Pour in the egg mixture and stir slowly over a gentle heat until scrambled. Stir in the tomato and remove from the heat.

Spread the toast with the remaining butter and pile the scrambled egg mixture on top. Serve immediately.

Serves 2

ACCOMPANIMENTS

When you plan a meal, you probably start by deciding upon a main dish – vegetarians do the same but build around this a whole host of interesting accompaniments to stretch the protein content be it eggs, cheese, vegetables, nuts or beans. These accompaniments may be pasta, pulses, bread or rice and grains. The choice is very wide if you consider pasta and noodles in all their guises; bread in umpteen varieties; rice and rice mixtures; and grains. Unusual grains worth considering include barley, buckwheat, bulgar and millet.

SPINACH EGGS

750 g (1½ lb) frozen leaf spinach, thawed and well drained
50 g (2 oz) butter
grated nutmeg
salt and pepper
4 eggs
4 tablespoons grated Double Gloucester cheese

Place the spinach and half the butter in a large pan. Add nutmeg, salt and pepper to taste.
Cook gently for 2 to 3 minutes until tender. Transfer to a shallow ovenproof dish.

Make 4 hollows in the spinach and carefully break an egg into each one. Sprinkle 1 tablespoon cheese over each egg and dot with the remaining butter.

Cook in a preheated moderate oven, 180°C (350°F), Gas Mark 4, for 15 minutes or until the eggs are cooked.

Sprinkle with pepper. Serve immediately, accompanied by wholemeal bread.

Serves 4

INDIVIDUAL CHEESE AND MUSHROOM SOUFFLÉS

25 g (1 oz) butter
50 g (2 oz) plain flour
300 ml (½ pint) milk
3 eggs, separated
175 g (6 oz) mushrooms, finely chopped
2 tablespoons chopped parsley
75 g (3 oz) Edam or Cheddar cheese, finely grated
½ teaspoon made mustard
salt and pepper

Place the butter, flour and milk in a saucepan and heat, whisking continuously until the sauce thickens. Cook for 2 minutes.

Cool slightly then beat in the egg yolks, mushrooms, parsley, cheese, mustard and salt and pepper to taste.

Whisk the egg whites until stiff and fold into the mixture. Divide between four individual greased soufflé dishes. Place in a preheated moderately hot oven, 190°C (375°F), Gas Mark 5, for 20 to 30 minutes or until well risen and golden brown. Serve immediately.

Serves 4

EGG, CORN AND PEPPER FRICASSÉE

8 eggs
50 g (2 oz) butter
3 tablespoons flour
300 ml (½ pint) milk
300 ml (½ pint) vegetable stock
1 × 340 g (11 oz) can sweetcorn with peppers
6 tablespoons cooked peas
salt and pepper
chopped parsley to garnish
toast triangles or croûtons to serve

Place the eggs in a pan of cold water. Bring to the boil and cook for 4 minutes. Drain and rinse in cold water then remove the shells. Keep warm in a bowl of hot water.

Place the butter, flour, milk and stock in a pan. Bring to the boil, whisking constantly and cook for 3 minutes. Add the sweetcorn and peppers, peas, drained eggs and salt and pepper to taste. Simmer gently for 2 to 3 minutes.

Spoon into a warmed serving dish and sprinkle with the parsley. Serve immediately with toasted triangles of bread or croûtons.

Serves 4

LEFT: *Onion and Tomato Scramble*

RIGHT: *Individual Cheese and Mushroom Soufflés*

Cheese Charlotte; Noodles Paprika

CHEESE CHARLOTTE

75 g (3 oz) butter
12 × 1 cm (½ inch) thick slices white bread, crusts removed
125 g (4 oz) mature Cheddar cheese, grated
350 ml (12 fl oz) milk
2 eggs, beaten
salt and pepper
pinch of mustard
2 tablespoons chopped chives

Spread the bread slices with the butter. Cut 4 or 5 slices into 2.5 cm (1 inch) wide fingers and use to line a deep, straight-sided casserole, buttered side against the casserole. Cut the remaining slices into cubes.

Make alternate layers of bread cubes and grated cheese in the casserole. Mix together the milk, eggs, salt and pepper to taste, mustard and chives and pour into the casserole.

Cook in a preheated moderate oven, 180°C (350°F), Gas Mark 4, for 30 minutes.

Serves 4

NOODLES PAPRIKA

175 g (6 oz) dried tagliatelle
salt and pepper
15 g (½ oz) butter
1 onion, finely chopped
1 clove garlic, crushed
2 teaspoons paprika
250 g (8 oz) cottage cheese
300 ml (½ pint) carton soured cream
few drops of Tabasco sauce
1 teaspoon caraway seeds (optional)
paprika to garnish

Cook the pasta according to the packet instructions. Drain well. Melt the butter in a frying pan, add the onion and garlic and fry until softened. Stir in the paprika. Cook, stirring, for 1 minute.

Remove from the heat and stir in the cottage cheese, soured cream, Tabasco and salt and pepper to taste. Add the caraway seeds (if using). Fold in the pasta.

Turn into a greased casserole and cook in a preheated moderate oven, 180°C (350°F), Gas Mark 4, for 30 minutes. Sprinkle with paprika to garnish.

Serves 4 to 6

ONION, CHEESE AND EGG BAKE

4 onions, chopped
salt and pepper
1 green pepper, cored, deseeded and chopped
300 g (10 oz) Cheddar cheese, grated
6 eggs
6 tablespoons milk
2 teaspoons coarse grain mustard

Cook the onion in lightly salted boiling water for 5 minutes. Drain, then place half in an ovenproof dish. Sprinkle with half the chopped pepper, then half the cheese. Repeat the layers.

Beat the remaining ingredients together, with salt and pepper to taste, pour into the casserole and cook in a preheated moderate oven, 180°C (350°F), Gas Mark 4, for 30 minutes. Serve with crusty bread.

Serves 4

WATERCRESS ROULADE

40 g (½ oz) butter
175 g (6 oz) watercress, chopped
4 eggs, separated
grated nutmeg
salt and pepper
FILLING:
15 g (½ oz) butter
1 onion, chopped
175 g (6 oz) button mushrooms, sliced
1 tablespoon wholmeal flour
142 ml (¼ pint) carton soured cream
2 tablespoons milk
1 tablespoon chopped parsley
2 tablespoons grated Parmesan cheese

Melt the butter in a pan and cook the watercress until it is soft. Place it in a bowl and add the egg yolks, beating well. Season to taste with nutmeg, salt and pepper. Whisk the egg whites until stiff and fold them into the watercress mixture.

Spread the mixture evenly into a lined and greased 30 × 20 cm (12 × 8 inch) Swiss roll tin. Cook in a preheated oven at 190°C, (375°F), Gas Mark 5 for 10–12 minutes.

FOR THE FILLING: melt the butter in a pan and fry the onion until soft. Add the mushrooms and cook for 3–4 minutes. Remove from the heat, stir in the flour and mix well. Cook for 1 minute, stirring. Add the milk and soured cream and cook until the sauce is thick and creamy. Stir in the parsley and season to taste with salt and pepper.

Sprinkle the cheese over a sheet of greaseproof paper. Turn out the roulade and peel off the lining paper. Spread with the filling and roll up. Serve immediately.

Serves 4–6

PIPERADE

2 tablespoons oil
1 large onion, sliced
1 red and 1 green pepper, cored, deseeded and sliced
2 cloves garlic, crushed
4 tomatoes, skinned and chopped
salt and pepper
4 eggs, beaten with 2 tablespoons milk

Heat the oil in a pan, add the onion and peppers and fry until softened. Add the garlic, tomatoes, and salt and pepper to taste. Simmer for 5 minutes, pour in the eggs and cook for 3 to 4 minutes, stirring occasionally.

Turn onto a warmed dish and serve immediately with crusty bread and a green salad.

Serves 2

Watercress Roulade; Piperade

FRIED APPLE AND CHEESE SANDWICHES

2 dessert apples, peeled, cored and grated
125 g (4 oz) Cheddar cheese, grated
1 × 113 g (4 oz) packet cream cheese
2 drops of Tabasco sauce
salt and pepper
8 slices wholemeal bread, buttered
50 g (2 oz) butter

Place the apple, Cheddar, cream cheese and Tabasco in a bowl. Mix until thoroughly blended. Season with salt and pepper to taste.

Divide the mixture between four of the bread slices and spread evenly. Cover with the remaining bread.

Melt half the butter in a frying pan. Add two of the sandwiches and fry gently on both sides until golden and the cheese has melted slightly. Repeat with the remaining butter and sandwiches. Serve immediately.

Serves 4

SAVOURY ONION PUFFS

25 g (1 oz) butter
375 g (12 oz) onions, chopped
175 g (6 oz) potatoes, boiled and diced
1 × 300 ml (7 fl oz) packet onion sauce mix
200 ml (1/3 pint) milk
125 g (4 oz) Cheddar cheese, grated
salt and pepper
212 g (7½ oz) frozen puff pastry, thawed
beaten egg to glaze

Melt the butter in a pan, add the onions and cook gently for 5 minutes. Add the potatoes.

Make up the sauce mix with the milk, as directed on the packet. Stir into the onion mixture with the cheese and salt and pepper to taste. Cook for 3 minutes.

Roll out the pastry on a lightly floured surface to a 30 cm (12 inch) square and cut into 4 squares. Place on a baking sheet.

Divide the onion mixture between the squares, placing it in the centre of each. Dampen the edges and fold the pastry over the filling to form triangular puffs. Press the edges together to seal, trim, knock up and flute. Brush the pastry with beaten egg.

Cook in a preheated hot oven, 220°C (425°F), Gas Mark 7, for 15 minutes until well risen and golden.

Serves 4

TOMATO FONDUE

50 g (2 oz) butter
1 small onion, finely chopped
2 cloves garlic, crushed
1 × 800 g (28 oz) can tomatoes
1 teaspoon dried oregano
1 teaspoon paprika
2 teaspoons dried basil
300 ml (½ pint) dry white wine
salt and pepper
500 g (1 lb) Cheddar cheese, grated
bread cubes to serve

Melt the butter in a fondue dish or flameproof casserole. Add the onion and garlic and fry until softened.

Drain the tomatoes thoroughly, then mash to a pulp. Add to the onion, with the oregano, paprika, basil and wine. Season with salt and pepper to taste. Cook gently for 10 minutes

Gradually stir in the cheese and cook over a low heat until melted. Check the seasoning. Serve immediately with the bread cubes. Dip these into the hot fondue before eating.

Serves 4

ENGLISH RAREBIT

50 g (2 oz) butter
300 ml (½ pint) beer
375 g (12 oz) mature Cheddar cheese
1½ tablespoons cornflour
1½ tablespoons coarse-grain mustard
salt and pepper
4 slices wholemeal bread, toasted and buttered
parsley sprigs to garnish

Melt the butter in a pan, add half the beer and the cheese. Heat gently until the cheese is melted.

Blend the cornflour with the remaining beer and add to the pan. Cook gently until the mixture thickens, then add the mustard and salt to taste.

Arrange the toast slices in a shallow flameproof dish and pour over the cheese mixture. Place under a preheated hot grill for 3 to 4 minutes until golden and bubbling.

Sprinkle with pepper to taste and garnish with parsley. Serve immediately.

Serves 4

CREAMY HERBED NOODLES

500 g (1 lb) dried tagliatelle
salt and pepper
50 g (2 oz) butter
1 small onion, chopped
1 clove garlic, crushed
284 ml (½ pint) carton single cream
250 ml (8 fl oz) dry white wine
2 tomatoes, skinned, deseeded and chopped
1 teaspoon green peppercorns
2 tablespoons chopped chives
4 mint leaves, chopped
4 tablespoons grated Double Gloucester cheese to serve

Cook the tagliatelle in plenty of boiling salted water.

Meanwhile, melt the butter in a small pan, add the onion and garlic and fry gently until soft and translucent. Add the cream, wine, tomatoes and peppercorns, and heat to just below boiling point. Simmer gently for 4 minutes.

Drain the noodles and place in a warmed serving dish. Add the chives and mint to the sauce. Check the seasoning. Pour over the noodles. Sprinkle with the cheese.

Serves 4

LEFT: *Savoury Onion Puffs; Tomato Fondue; Fried Apple and Cheese Sandwiches*
RIGHT: *English Rarebit; Creamy Herbed Noodles; Egg and Onion Casserole*

EGG AND ONION CASSEROLE

25 g (1 oz) butter
300 ml (½ pint) milk
2 small onions, finely chopped
1 × 300 ml (½ pint) packet onion sauce mix
4 hard-boiled eggs, roughly chopped
4 tablespoons fresh white breadcrumbs

Melt the butter in a pan, add the milk and onions and bring slowly to the boil. Lower the heat, cover and simmer for 4 minutes.

Cool slightly, then gradually stir into the onion sauce mix. Return to the heat and cook until thickened.

Stir in the egg, pour into a small casserole dish and cover with the breadcrumbs.

Place under a preheated hot grill for 3 minutes or until the crumbs are crisp and golden.

Serves 4

DEVILLED SCRAMBLE AND BEANS

15 g (½ oz) butter
1 onion, finely chopped
1 clove garlic, crushed
6 eggs
3 tablespoons milk
1 tablespoon tomato ketchup
½ teaspoon made mustard
salt and pepper
1 × 447 g (15 oz) can baked beans
chopped parsley to garnish

Melt the butter in a pan, add the onion and garlic and fry until soft.

Beat together the eggs, milk, tomato ketchup, mustard and salt and pepper to taste. Add to the pan and cook over a medium heat, stirring gently, until the mixture is set but still soft.

Heat the baked beans and arrange in a circle on a hot serving dish. Pile the scrambled egg into the centre and sprinkle with chopped parsley. Serve immediately.

Serves 4

Devilled Scramble and Beans

CRUNCHY TOPPED TOAST

4 slices bread
150 g (5 oz) Cheddar cheese, grated
25 g (1 oz) peanuts, chopped
2 small dessert apples, peeled, cored and grated
1 teaspoon lemon juice
1 drop of Tabasco sauce
salt and pepper
parsley sprigs to garnish

Toast the bread lightly on both sides.

Mix together the remaining ingredients, with salt and pepper to taste, then spread over the toast. Place under a preheated moderate grill for about 5 minutes until the cheese is bubbling and golden. Serve immediately, garnished with parsley.

Serves 4

HAWAIIAN TOAST

4 slices bread
150 g (5 oz) carton natural low-fat yogurt
125 g (4 oz) Double Gloucester cheese, grated
½ green pepper, cored, deseeded and chopped
5 pineapple rings
salt and pepper
parsley sprigs to garnish

Toast the bread lightly on both sides.

Mix together the yogurt, cheese, green pepper and 1 chopped pineapple ring. Add salt and pepper to taste. Spread the mixture over the toast and top each with a pineapple ring.

Place under a preheated moderate grill for 4 to 6 minutes or until the cheese begins to bubble and brown.

Serve hot, garnished with a parsley sprig inside each pineapple ring.

Serves 4

CAULIFLOWER CHEESE BAKE

1 cauliflower divided into florets
salt and pepper
150 ml (¼ pint) milk
1 egg, beaten
75 g (3 oz) cheese, grated
2 teaspoons paprika
1 tomato, sliced, to garnish

Cook the cauliflower in boiling salted water for 5 minutes, then drain.

Beat together the milk, egg, 50 g (2 oz) of the cheese, paprika and salt and pepper to taste.

Place the cauliflower in a lightly greased 1.5 litre (2½ pint) ovenproof dish. Pour the egg mixture over the cauliflower and sprinkle with the remaining cheese. Cook in a preheated moderate oven, 180°C (350°F), Gas Mark 4, for 30 to 40 minutes or until the cheese custard is set. Garnish with tomato slices.

Serves 4

STILTON EGGS

4 tablespoons frozen mixed vegetables, cooked
75 g (3 oz) Stilton cheese, crumbled
4 eggs
salt and pepper
2 tablespoons milk
parsley sprigs to garnish

Place the mixed vegetables in 4 small, lightly greased ovenproof dishes. Sprinkle 50 g (2 oz) of the cheese over the top.

Break an egg into each dish and sprinkle with salt and pepper. Spoon the milk over the top and sprinkle with the remaining cheese.

Place the dishes in a roasting tin, half-filled with water. Cook in a preheated moderately hot oven, 190°C (375°F), Gas Mark 5, for 15 minutes or until the eggs are set. Garnish with parsley and serve with crispbreads.

Serves 4

Cauliflower Cheese Bake; Stilton Eggs

DESSERTS

Whether you are looking for a simple fruit salad to round off an informal or family meal or an impressive cream, fruit and nut torte to crown a perfect celebratory meal, you'll find lots of ideas here.

Many contain nutritious nuts, eggs, fruit and cheese that help to boost the vegetarian's intake of proteins, minerals and vitamins; while some are purely indulgent with their lashings of cream, chocolate and caramel.

Agar-agar and vegetable gel powder has been suggested for those moulded desserts usually made with gelatine. Both are tasteless, and easy to use. Follow the recipe instructions and packet instructions for use.

Some meals are, of course, sufficient without desserts. In such cases, a vegetarian cheese and piece of fruit make ideal finishing partners. Choose from the wide selection of new vegetarian cheeses including Cheshire, Cheddar and Double Gloucester. Let nature take the guiding hand with your choice of fruits from early spring apricots and gooseberries; summer berry and tree fruits like raspberries, strawberries, peaches, figs and nectarines; mellow autumn windfall and hedgerow fruits like apples, pears and blackberries; to imported winter and festive fruits like satsumas, clementines, grapes, kiwi and pomegranates.

BLACKBERRY AND APPLE WHIP

500 g (1 lb) fresh blackberries
3 tablespoons caster sugar
1 × 128 g (4 oz) jar apple purée (see note)
2 tablespoons apple juice concentrate (optional)
300 ml (½ pint) double cream
mint sprigs, to decorate

Set aside 8 of the blackberries for decoration. Place the remainder in a saucepan with 1-2 tablespoons of caster sugar and heat gently until softened. Leave to cool slightly then puree in a blender. Pour the puree into a mixing bowl and whisk in the apple puree. Add the apple juice concentrate, if liked. Chill in the refrigerator for 1 hour.

Whip the cream with the remaining sugar until thick and fold half into the fruit purée. Spoon the mixture into 4 glass sundae dishes. Place a heaped tablespoon of the remaining cream on each whip. Decorate with the reserved blackberries and a sprig of mint. Serve immediately.

Serves 4

NOTE: Apple puree in the baby food range is ideal for this recipe.

SUMMER PUDDING

1 kg (2 lb) mixed summer fruits, e.g. blackcurrants, raspberries, redcurrants
175-250 g (6–8 oz) sugar
12 trifle sponges

Put the fruits in a large saucepan, cover and bring slowly to the boil. Simmer for 7 to 10 minutes. Remove from the heat, stir in the sugar to taste and leave to cool.

Slice the sponge cakes in half lengthways and use to line the base and sides of a 1.5 litre (2½ pint) pudding basin. Spoon in three quarters of the stewed fruit and top with the remaining sponge cakes. Spoon over a little more fruit. Cover with a saucer or plate, gently pushing down. Leave in the refrigerator overnight.

Remove the plate, run a palette knife around the edge of the pudding and turn out onto a deep serving plate. Spoon over the remaining fruit and serve with whipped cream.

Serves 10

Hazelnut and Raspberry Torte

250 g (8 oz) hazelnuts
150 g (5 oz) plain flour
salt
125 g (4 oz) icing sugar, sifted
125 g (4 oz) butter softened
1 egg yolk
FILLING:
284 ml (½ pint) carton whipping cream, whipped
75 g (3 oz) cranberry sauce
250 g (8 oz) fresh raspberries
TO DECORATE:
125 ml (4 fl oz) double cream, whipped
whole raspberries
hazelnuts, toasted

Place the hazelnuts under a hot grill for a few minutes to brown. Remove the skins and grind coarsely.

Sift the flour and a pinch of salt on to a board. Make a well in the centre, put in the hazelnuts, icing sugar, butter and egg yolk. Work the flour into the centre, using the fingertips, and mix to a smooth paste. Cover and chill for 1 hour.

Divide the dough into 4. Roll out each piece into a 20 cm (8 inch) circle and place on lightly greased baking sheets. Prick each circle with a fork and chill for 1 hour.

Bake in a preheated moderately hot oven, 190°C (375°F), Gas Mark 5, for 8 to 10 minutes, until golden. Cool on wire racks.

Place one round on a serving plate. Mix together the whipped cream and cranberry sauce and use a third to cover the biscuit base. Cover with a third of the raspberries and place another biscuit round on top. Repeat the layers twice more, finishing with a biscuit round.

Spread half the whipped cream in a thin layer over the top of the torte; use the remaining cream to pipe rosettes around the edge. Finish with raspberries and hazelnuts.

Serves 12

LEFT: *Berry Ice Cream; Summer Pudding*

RIGHT: *Hazelnut and Raspberry Torte; Choc-Orange Mousse*

Choc-Orange Mousse

375 g (12 oz) plain chocolate
40 g (1½ oz) butter
6 eggs, separated
grated rind and juice of 2 oranges
2 tablespoons brandy
TO DECORATE:
142 ml (¼ pint) carton double cream, whipped
2 chocolate flakes, broken into pieces

Break the chocolate into a heatproof bowl over a pan of hot water. Stir occasionally until melted, then stir in the butter and blend well. Add the egg yolks and mix well. Remove from the heat. Stir in the orange rind and juice and the brandy.

Whisk the egg whites until very stiff and fold into the chocolate mixture. Transfer to a serving dish and chill for 3 hours.

Decorate with whipped cream and chocolate flake to serve.

Serves 10 to 12

CANTELOUPE CUPS

3 small cantaloupe melons
500 g (1 lb) ripe plums, sliced
1 × 411 g (14 oz) can black cherries, drained and pitted
200 ml (7 fl oz) creme fraîche
2 tablespoons flaked almonds, lightly toasted.

Chill the melons for 1-2 hours before serving. Cut them in half horizontally and scoop out the pips. Place on six individual dishes. Place the plums and cherries in a bowl and mix lightly. Spoon into the melon cups and top each with creme fraîche. Scatter over the toasted almond flakes and serve immediately.
Serves 6

PAVLOVA

4 egg whites
250 g (8 oz) caster sugar
1 teaspoon white wine vinegar
2 teaspoons cornflour
FILLING:
284 ml (½ pint) carton double cream, whipped
2 ripe nectarines, thinly sliced
250 g (8 oz) fresh raspberries
125 g (4 oz) red currants
2 tablespoons redcurrant jelly

Place the egg whites in a clean bowl and whisk until they form stiff peaks. Sprinkle over 2 teaspoons of sugar and whisk well. Gradually add half the remaining sugar, the vinegar and the cornflour, whisking between each addition.

Fold in the remaining sugar. Spoon or pipe the meringue onto a baking sheet lined with baking parchment to make a 23 cm/9 inch round with a slight hollow in the centre. Bake at 140°C (275°F) Gas Mark 1 for about 1½ hours or until crisp.

Remove the meringue from the paper and place in a serving dish. Spoon the whipped cream into the centre and arrange the fruit on top. Warm the redcurrant jelly and spoon it over the fruit. Keep cool if not served immediately. Pavlova must be served on the day it is made.
Serves 4–6

RICOTTA CHEESE CAKE

500 g (1 lb) ricotta cheese, drained
150 g (5 oz) caster sugar
7 eggs, separated
150 g (5 oz) ground almonds
1 tablespoon grated lemon rind
2 tablespoons cornflour
icing sugar, to decorate

Place the ricotta cheese in a mixing bowl with the sugar and beat well until creamy. Add the egg yolks one by one, beating well each time. Stir in the ground almonds and grated lemon rind.

Whisk the egg whites until stiff. Fold half the whites into the cheese mixture. Sift in the cornflour and fold it in with the remaining meringue. Pour the mixture into a greased 25 cm (10 inch) springform tin lined with baking parchment. Bake at 180°C (350°F) Gas Mark 4 for 50 minutes.

Allow the cake to cool in the tin, then remove it carefully and place in a serving dish. Sift icing sugar over the top and serve.
Serves 8

GINGER AND MARMALADE DREAMS

125 g (4 oz) medium-fat curd cheese
½ teaspoon ground ginger
2 tablespoons coarse-cut marmalade
2 tablespoons orange juice
1 tablespoon brandy
142 ml (¼ pint) carton double cream
stem ginger to decorate

Place the cheese in a bowl and blend in the ginger, marmalade, orange juice and brandy. Whip the cream until it just holds its shape, then gently fold into the cheese mixture.

Spoon into 4 glass dishes and decorate with ginger. Chill before serving, with brandy snaps if liked.
Serves 4

RIGHT: *Mocha Dessert; Ginger and Nut Ice Cream*

MOCHA DESSERT

2-3 tablespoons cornflour
a pinch of salt
3-4 tablespoons caster sugar
2 tablespoons cocoa powder
300 ml (½ pint) milk
300 ml (½ pint) coffee
2 drops of vanilla essence
15 g (½ oz) unsalted butter
chocolate curls, to decorate (see note)

Mix the cornflour, salt, sugar and cocoa powder to a smooth paste with a little milk. Mix the remaining milk with the coffee, heat to boiling point and pour over the paste, stirring constantly. Return to a clean pan and cook, still stirring, until the mixture boils. Reduce the heat and cook gently for 10 minutes. Add the vanilla essence and butter. Allow to cool before spooning into individual serving dishes. Serve cold, decorated with chocolate curls.

NOTE: To make chocolate curls, shave slivers from a chocolate block, using a potato peeler.

Serves 4

GINGER AND NUT ICE CREAM

142 ml (¼ pint) carton double cream
1 tablespoon milk
2 tablespoons icing sugar, sifted
25 g (1 oz) preserved ginger, finely chopped
2 teaspoons ginger syrup
1-2 tablespoons finely chopped hazelnuts

Place the cream and milk in a bowl and whip lightly. Fold in the icing sugar. Pour into a shallow freezer tray, cover and freeze for about 45 minutes, until the ice cream has frozen around the sides of the tray.

Turn into a chilled bowl and whisk until smooth. Stir in the ginger, syrup and hazelnuts.

Return the ice cream to the tray, cover and freeze until firm. Transfer to the refrigerator about 20 minutes before serving to soften. Scoop into dishes. Serve with crisp biscuits.

Serves 2

ORANGE AND PINEAPPLE JELLY

175 ml (6 fl oz) orange juice
175 ml (6 fl oz) pineapple juice
2 teaspoons agar-agar powder
150 g (5 oz) carton natural yogurt
orange twists to decorate

Mix the juices together then whisk in the agar-agar. Bring to the boil and cook until the agar has dissolved. Pour into a bowl and place in the refrigerator until just beginning to set.

Whisk in the yogurt until well blended, then pour into 4 glass serving dishes. Leave until set, then decorate with orange twists.
Serves 4

FRUITS IN SYRUP

1 Ogen melon
250 g (8 oz) black grapes
250 g (8 oz) strawberries
4 tablespoons apricot preserve, sieved
4 tablespoons dry white wine
150 g (5 oz) Greek-style yogurt
preserved ginger, to decorate (optional)

Cut the melon in half, remove the seeds, and cut the flesh into cubes. Place in a serving dish. Slice the grapes and remove the pips. Clean and slice the strawberries. Lightly mix the fruits together.

Warm the apricot preserve over a low heat, add the wine and blend together. Pour over the fruit. Spoon the yogurt on top and serve lightly chilled, decorated with slices of preserved ginger if liked.
Serves 4

LEFT: *Orange and Pineapple Jelly; Fruits in Syrup*

RIGHT: *Hazelnut and Fruit Torte*

ORANGE MOUSSE

6 eggs, separated
175 g (6 oz) caster sugar
3 tablespoons Cointreau or orange liqueur
2 teaspoons agar-agar
grated rind and juice of 4 oranges
142 ml (¼ pint) carton double cream, lightly whipped
mint leaves to decorate

Put the egg yolks and sugar in a bowl over a pan of hot water and whisk until thick and creamy. Gradually whisk in the Cointreau. Mix the agar-agar with the orange juice and boil for 2 minutes. Add to mousse mixture and continue whisking until the mixture is thick. Remove from the heat and allow to cool slightly. cool slightly.

Fold in the cream. Whisk the egg whites until stiff and fold into the orange mixture.

Spoon into individual dishes and chill until set.

Decorate with mint to serve.

Serve 6

BROWN BREAD ICE CREAM

75 g (3 oz) wholemeal breadcrumbs
150 g (5 oz) light muscovado sugar
50 g (2 oz) hazelnuts, chopped
3 egg whites
284 ml (½ pint) carton double cream
chopped hazelnuts to decorate (optional)

Mix the breadcrumbs with 50 g (2 oz) of the sugar and the hazelnuts. Sprinkle onto a baking sheet and cook under a medium grill until crisp, turning frequently. Allow to cool.

Whisk the egg whites until they stand in stiff peaks then gently stir in the remaining sugar. Whip the cream until it stands in soft peaks and fold into the egg white mixture. Fold in the toasted breadcrumb mixture. Pour into a freezerproof container and freeze for at least 2 hours.

Serve scooped into glasses and topped with a few extra chopped hazelnuts if liked.

Serves 6

HAZELNUT AND FRUIT TORTE

PASTRY:
150 g (5 oz) plain flour
pinch of salt
250 g (8 oz) hazelnuts, ground
125 g (4 oz) caster sugar
125 g (4 oz) butter, softened
1 egg yolk

FILLING:
284 ml (½ pint) carton double cream, whipped
1 fresh pineapple, peeled, cored and sliced

Sift the flour and salt onto a board, make a well in the centre and put in the hazelnuts, sugar, butter and egg yolk. Work the flour into the centre, using the fingers; mix to a smooth paste. Cover and chill for 1 hour.

Divide the dough into 3 pieces. Roll out each piece and use to line the bases of three 20 cm (8 inch) flan rings, place on baking sheets. Prick with a fork. Mark one round into 8 triangles. Bake in a preheated moderately hot oven, 190°C (375°F), Gas Mark 5, for 10 minutes or until golden brown. Break the marked round into triangles. Cool.

Put one circle on a serving dish and spread with a layer of cream. Top with half the pineapple, cover with the other round and spread with cream.

Decorate with the remaining cream: pipe 8 lines radiating from the centre, place the pastry triangles on these and top with the remaining pineapple. Finish with cream rosettes.

Serves 8

CUSTARD

Custard powder is an invaluable store-cupboard stand-by, but it is useful to be able to make your own as a luxurious alternative when time permits.

For 600 ml (1 pint), you will need 600 ml/1 pint milk, 2 tablespoons of caster sugar, a vanilla pod and 4 egg yolks. Heat the milk with the vanilla pod without letting it boil. Remove from the heat and leave to stand for 10 minutes. Discard the vanilla pod. Whisk the egg yolks in a bowl. Slowly pour on the hot milk, stirring constantly. Strain the custard into a double saucepan with hot water in the lower pan or, a bowl set over a pan filled with hot water. Do not let the water boil. Stir over a very low heat until thick and creamy.

Use hot to pour over puddings. If you wish to use it cold, sprinkle with sugar to prevent a skin forming.

If custard is cooked over too high a heat the egg yolks will curdle. Be patient and keep stirring over very low heat.

APPLE TRIFLE

5 trifle sponges
3 tablespoons apricot conserve
4 dessert apples, peeled, cored and sliced
50 g (2 oz) custard powder
600 ml (1 pint) milk
1 egg yolk
25 g (1 oz) caster sugar
284 ml (½ pint) carton double cream
chopped hazelnuts, to decorate

Slice the sponges in half and spread with apricot conserve. Arrange in the bottom of a deep 1.75 litre/3 pint serving bowl.

Poach the sliced apples in a little water until just soft. Cool and spoon over the sponge. Use the custard powder, milk, egg yolk and sugar to make up the custard as for Custard Cream Fritters (right). Let it cool slightly before pouring over the apples. Leave in a cool place to set quite firm.

Beat the cream until thick and spoon over the custard. Scatter chopped nuts on top and serve.

Serves 6-8

CUSTARD CREAM FRITTERS

50 g (2 oz) custard powder
300 ml (½ pint) single cream or milk
2 egg yolks
25 g (1 oz) caster sugar
½ teaspoon vanilla essence, or 2-3 teaspoons dark rum or orange liqueur
1 egg white
50 g (2 oz) very fine fresh white breadcrumbs
50 g (2 oz) butter

Put the custard powder in a heavy-based pan and blend with a little of the cream or milk to make a thin paste. Stir in the remaining cream or milk.

Bring slowly to the boil, stirring, until very thick. Remove from the heat.

Beat in the egg yolks and the sugar. Continue beating until the mixture is cool. Beat in the flavouring and pour into a shallow 15 cm (6 inch) round dish. Set aside until cold and very stiff.

Brush with the egg white and sprinkle with the breadcrumbs until well coated, pressing on gently.

Melt the butter in an 18 cm (7 inch) heavy-based frying pan over a fairly high heat: the butter must be really hot and frothy but not brown.

Fry for about 2 minutes on each side until crisp and golden.

Drain well and cut the mixture into 6 pieces.

Serve warm with melted apricot jam or honey.

Makes 6

RASPBERRY GÂTEAU

SPONGE BASE:
2 eggs
50 g (2 oz) caster sugar
50 g (2 oz) plain flour, sifted
1 tablespoon dry sherry
TOPPING:
142 ml (¼ pint) carton soured cream
150 g (5 oz) raspberry yogurt
250 g (8 oz) raspberries
TO DECORATE:
125 g (4 oz) raspberries
25 g (1 oz) caster sugar

Grease and line a 20 cm (8 inch) sandwich tin with greased, greaseproof paper.

Put the eggs and sugar in a bowl, place over a pan of hot water and whisk until the mixture is pale in colour and thick enough to leave a trail with the whisk. Remove the bowl from the pan and continue whisking until the mixture is cool.

Quickly fold in the flour with a metal spoon. Pour into the prepared tin and bake in a preheated moderately hot oven, 190°C (375°F), Gas Mark 5, for 15 to 20 minutes until the sponge springs back when pressed lightly.

Leave in the tin for 5 minutes then cool on a wire rack. Place the sponge on a serving plate, prick all over and sprinkle with the sherry.

For the topping: mix together the cream and yogurt. Fold in the raspberries and pile the mixture onto the sponge. Decorate with raspberries and sprinkle with caster sugar. Chill.

Serves 6

BURNT BRAMBLE CREAMS

500 g (1 lb) blackberries
1 tablespoon water
2 tablespoons sugar
15 g (½ oz) flaked almonds
CUSTARD
50 g (2 oz) custard powder
284 ml (½ pint) single cream
2 egg yolks
25 g (1 oz) caster sugar
2 drops vanilla essence

Poach the blackberries with the water and 1 tablespoon sugar until just soft. Drain and divide between 4 heatproof individual dishes. Chill in the refrigerator.

Make the custard as for Custard Cream Fritters (p. 122) and pour over the fruit. Sprinkle with the remaining sugar and the flaked almonds and place under a preheated grill until the sugar has melted and the almonds nicely browned. Serve immediately.

Serves 4

Raspberry Gâteau; Burnt Bramble Creams

VANILLA RICE CREAMS

50 g (2 oz) pudding rice
475 ml (16 fl oz) milk
50 g (2 oz) sugar
2 eggs, separated
1 teaspoon vanilla essence
142 ml (¼ pint) carton double cream, whipped
TO DECORATE:
50 g (2 oz) crushed peanut brittle

Place the rice in a heavy-based pan. Add the milk and sugar and bring to the boil, stirring constantly. Cover and cook over very low heat for 40 to 45 minutes, stirring occasionally, until all the milk has been absorbed and the rice is soft.

Beat in the egg yolks, one at a time, and return to the heat for 1 minute, without boiling, stirring constantly. Beat in the vanilla essence. Sieve or work in a blender or food processor until smooth; cool.

Whisk the egg whites until stiff. Fold together the egg whites, rice mixture and cream. Spoon into individual serving dishes and chill.

Sprinkle with peanut brittle to serve.

Serves 6

NOTE: For a speedy version, heat 1 × 450 g (15 oz) can creamed rice, then beat in the egg yolks and proceed as above.

BUTTERSCOTCH NUT PIE

25 g (1 oz) butter
6 digestive biscuits, crushed
200 ml (7 fl oz) milk
125 ml (4 fl oz) single cream
1 × 69 g (3 oz) packet butterscotch dessert whip
50 g (2 oz) hazelnuts, toasted and chopped
TO DECORATE:
142 ml (¼ pint) carton double cream, whipped
hazelnuts, toasted

Melt the butter and stir in the biscuit crumbs. Press into the base of a 15 cm (6 inch) flan dish.

Gradually add the milk and cream to the butterscotch whip, mixing until smooth. Add the hazelnuts and pile on top of the biscuit base.

Decorate with whipped cream and hazelnuts just before serving.

Serves 4

BAKED BANANAS

2 bananas, thickly sliced
2 teaspoons lemon juice
25 g (1 oz) dates, chopped
2 teaspoons clear honey
1 tablespoon water
1-2 tablespoons chopped walnuts

Place the bananas in a 450 ml (¾ pint) ovenproof dish, add the lemon juice and toss well. Sprinkle the dates over the top.

Blend together the honey and water and spoon over the bananas. Top with the walnuts. Cover with foil and cook in a preheated moderate oven, 180°C (350°F), Gas Mark 4, for 20 minutes. Serve hot, with cream.

Serves 2

Vanilla Rice Creams

LAYERED FRUIT JELLY

1 × 227 g (8 oz) can pineapple pieces
4 teaspoons agar-agar powder
2 bananas
juice of 1 lemon
125 g (4 oz) raspberries
125 g (4 oz) cherries, stoned

Drain the pineapple, reserving the juice. Add water to the juice to make up to 600 ml (1 pint). Whisk in the agar-agar, bring to the boil and cook until the agar has dissolved.

Slice the bananas and sprinkle with the lemon juice. Set aside with the pineapple, banana, raspberries and cherries.

Pour about 2.5 cm (1 inch) of the jelly into a dampened mould (or individual moulds) and arrange the bananas in the jelly. Allow to set, then add another layer of jelly and arrange another layer of fruit in this.

Repeat the layers until all the ingredients are used up, being sure to allow the jelly to set each time. When the jelly is completely set, turn out onto a plate to serve.

Serves 6

FLUFFY ORANGE PUDDING

juice and grated rind of 1 orange
50 g (2 oz) butter, softened
125 g (4 oz) caster sugar
300 ml (½ pint) milk
50 g (2 oz) self-raising flour
2 eggs, separated

Put all the ingredients, except the egg whites, into a blender or food processor and blend until smooth.

Alternatively, put the orange juice and rind, butter and sugar in a bowl and beat until light and fluffy, then gradually stir in the milk. Whisk the egg whites until stiff, then fold into the mixture.

Turn into a greased 1 litre (1¾ pint) ovenproof dish and place in a roasting tin containing enough water to come halfway up the sides of the dish.

Cook in a preheated moderately hot oven, 190°C (375°F), Gas Mark 5, for 50 minutes.

Serves 4

RASPBERRY FOOL

385 g (13 oz) can raspberries in syrup
150 ml (¼ pint) custard, cooled
175 ml (6 fl oz) double cream, whipped
sponge fingers to serve

Drain the raspberries, reserving the syrup and a few raspberries for decoration. Purée the rest by rubbing through a sieve or working in a blender, adding a little of the syrup if necessary. Fold in the custard and cream.

Pour into 4 glass serving dishes and top with the reserved raspberries. Chill before serving, with sponge fingers.

Serves 4

Layered Fruit Jelly; Raspberry Fool

Plum Tart

PLUM TART

125 g (4 oz) plain flour
pinch of salt
1 teaspoon caster sugar
75 g (3 oz) butter
1 egg, beaten
FILLING:
250 g (8 oz) red plums, halved and stoned
150 ml (1/4 pint) water
50 g (2 oz) sugar
2 teaspoons cornflour
TO FINISH:
sifted icing sugar

Sift the flour and salt into a bowl and add the sugar. Rub in the butter until the mixture resembles breadcrumbs. Add the egg and mix to a smooth dough. Knead lightly, cover and chill for 30 minutes.

Roll out the dough on a floured surface and use to line a 15 cm (6 inch) flan ring placed on a baking sheet. Reserve the trimmings.

Put the plums, water and sugar in a saucepan. Cook gently until tender. Drain, reserving the juice.

Blend the cornflour with a little cooled juice, then add the remainder. Bring to the boil, stirring. Add the plums and spoon into the pastry case. Cut strips from the pastry trimmings and make a lattice pattern over the filling.

Cook in a preheated moderately hot oven, 200°C (400°F), Gas Mark 6, for 25 minutes. Cool in the tin.

When cold, transfer to a serving plate and sprinkle with icing sugar.

Serves 2-3

CORINTHIAN COFFEE CAKE

175 g (6 oz) butter
175 g (6 oz) caster sugar
3 eggs, beaten
175 g (6 oz) self-raising flour, sifted
TO SERVE:
300 ml (1/2 pint) strong black coffee, sweetened
4 tablespoons brandy
284 ml (1/2 pint) carton double cream, whipped
fruit or nuts to decorate

Cream the butter and sugar until light. Gradually beat in the eggs, then fold in the flour. Turn into a greased and floured 23 cm (9 inch) ring tin and bake in a preheated moderately hot oven, 190°C (375°F), Gas Mark 5, for about 25 minutes, until well risen. Cool on a wire rack.

Mix the coffee and brandy together and spoon over the cake. Cover with whipped cream and decorate with fruit or nuts.

Serves 4 to 6

FLORIDA SALAD

3 pink grapefruit
3 white grapefruit
6 oranges
1 cantaloupe melon
175 g (6 oz) caster sugar
2 tablespoons lemon juice

Peel the citrus fruits and remove the segments with a sharp knife, discarding all pith. Place in a serving bowl. Halve the melon and remove the seeds. Cut the flesh into neat cubes and add to the bowl. Sprinkle with the caster sugar and lemon juice and chill before serving.

Serves 12

LEMON TART

PASTRY:
175 g (6 oz) plain flour
2 tablespoons caster sugar
125 g (4 oz) cold butter, cut into small pieces
1 egg yolk
FILLING:
175 g (6 oz) sugar
150 ml (¼ pint) fresh lemon juice
125 ml (4 fl oz) orange juice
grated zest of 3 lemons
4 eggs
50 g (2 oz) butter
4 tablespoons double cream
TO FINISH:
2 lemons, cut into segments
icing sugar, sifted

Sift the flour onto a board and stir in the sugar. Make a hollow in the centre and add the butter and egg yolk. Using the fingertips, lightly bring the flour mixture into the centre over the butter and egg to combine the ingredients. Knead lightly and form into a ball. Dust with flour, cover with clingfilm and chill for 1 hour.

Roll out the dough and use to line a 25 cm (10 inch) flan tin with a removable base. Prick with a fork and chill for 1 hour. Line the pastry case with greaseproof paper and dried beans and bake in a preheated moderately hot oven, 200°C (400°F), Gas Mark 6, for 10 to 15 minutes, until lightly browned. Remove the greaseproof paper and baking beans.

Place the sugar, lemon and orange juice, zest and eggs in a bowl and beat together. Melt the butter in a pan, stir in the cream, add the egg mixture and cook over a low heat, stirring, until thickened; take care not to scramble the eggs and do not boil. Remove from the heat, transfer to a bowl and cover the surface with dampened greaseproof paper. Cover the bowl with clingfilm and leave to cool.

Spoon the custard into the pastry case and bake in a preheated moderately hot oven, 190°C (375°F), Gas Mark 5, for 20 minutes.

Arrange the lemon segments on top and sprinkle liberally with icing sugar. Place under a preheated hot grill for 1 minute until golden brown. Serve warm or cold with cream.

Serves 10 to 12

ICED CHOCOLATE TERRINE

75 g (3 oz) pitted dates, finely chopped
juice 1 large orange
3 tablepoons medium or sweet sherry
300 ml (½ pint) double cream
200 g (7 oz) plain chocolate
50 g (2 oz) butter
1 egg yolk
2 egg whites
2 teaspoons caster sugar

Place the dates in a bowl, pour on the orange juice and sherry, cover and leave to soak for at least 1 hour.

Whip the cream until it holds soft peaks. Spread half of it on the base and sides of a 600 ml (1 pint) loaf tin or plastic box. Place in the freezer while you complete the dessert. Place the reserved cream in the refrigerator.

Break the chocolate into squares and reserve 25 g (1 oz). Melt the remaining chocolate with the butter in the top of a double boiler or a bowl over a pan of simmering water. Do not allow the water to touch the base of the bowl, or the chocolate may become too hot. Remove the bowl from the heat and stir in the egg yolks, the soaked dates and the liquid.

Whisk the egg whites until they form glossy peaks, sprinkle on the sugar and whisk again.

Stir the reserved cream into the chocolate mixture, and fold in the egg whites.

Pour the mixture into the cream-lined container, cover and freeze for about 4 hours.

Grate the reserved chocolate.

To serve, dip the container briefly in hot water, run a knife around the sides and turn it out on to a dish.

Sprinkle on the grated chocolate to decorate.

Serves 6

MINCEMEAT BAKED APPLES

4 × 150 g (5 oz) cooking apples
50 g (2 oz) vegetarian mincemeat
150 ml (¼ pint) apple juice
4 tablespoons single cream (optional)

Remove the core from the apples and score the skin around the middle. Fill the centre with the mincemeat.

Place in a shallow ovenproof dish and pour the apple juice over. Bake in a preheated moderately hot oven, 190°C (375°F), Gas Mark 5, for 30 minutes or until the apples are soft. Serve with the cream, if using.

Serves 4

RHUBARB CRUNCH

500 g (1 lb) rhubarb, chopped
grated rind and juice of 1 orange
about 50 g (2 oz) sugar
150 g (5 oz) mandarin yogurt
4 digestive biscuits, crushed
¼ teaspoon mixed spice
2 slices orange to decorate

Place the rhubarb in a pan with the orange rind and juice. Stew until the fruit is soft, then add sugar to taste. Leave to cool.

Place the fruit in a blender or pass through a sieve to make a purée. Stir in the yogurt and spoon the mixture into 4 glass serving dishes.

Mix the biscuits with the mixed spice and spoon over the fruit. Chill in the refrigerator until required.

Cut the orange slices into quarters and use 2 to decorate each crunch.

Serves 4

RASPBERRY AND PEACH PANCAKES

PANCAKES:
125 g (4 oz) plain flour
pinch of salt
1 egg
300 ml (½ pint) milk
15 g (½ oz) butter for frying
FILLING:
4 peaches, stoned and sliced
175 g (6 oz) raspberries
1 tablespoon water
1-2 teaspoons sugar
TO DECORATE:
sifted icing sugar

Sift the flour and salt into a bowl. Make a well in the centre and add the egg and half the milk. Beat smooth, then stir in the remaining milk.

Lightly grease an 18 cm (7 inch) non-stick frying pan with the butter and place over moderate heat. Pour in enough batter to cover the base of the pan. Cook until the underside is browned, then toss or turn and cook the other side.

Repeat with the remaining batter to make 8 pancakes; stack them on a plate, with a piece of greaseproof paper between each one, over a pan of simmering water to keep hot.

Place the peaches in a pan with the raspberries and water. Cook gently until the peaches are soft. Add 1-2 teaspoons sugar to taste. Divide the filling between the pancakes and roll or fold. Arrange on a warm serving dish and sprinkle with icing sugar.

Serves 4

Mincemeat Baked Apples; Raspberry and Peach Pancakes; Rhubarb Crunch

SPICY FRUIT SALAD

125 g (4 oz) apricots
150 ml (¼ pint) orange juice
1 tablespoon clear honey
a pinch of ground cinnamon
25 g (1 oz) raisins
2 bananas
2 teaspoons lemon juice
150 g (5 oz) carton natural yogurt
grated nutmeg

Soak the apricots in cold water overnight. Drain and place in a small heavy saucepan with the orange juice, honey, cinnamon and raisins. Cook over a gentle heat until soft, but do not let the apricots become mushy.

Allow to cool slightly. Slice the bananas and toss in the lemon juice. Combine with the apricots and raisins.

Divide the fruit between 4 serving dishes. Spoon the yogurt over the fruit and sprinkle with grated nutmeg. Chill before serving.

Serves 4

GOOSEBERRY SNOW

50 g (2 oz) unsalted butter
500 g (1 lb) gooseberries, topped and tailed
2 tablespoons demerara sugar
2 egg whites
125 g (4 oz) caster sugar

Melt the butter in a heavy-bottomed pan which will hold the gooseberries in a single layer. Add the sugar and stir till dissolved. Add the gooseberries, cover and cook gently until they change colour but are still whole. Allow to cool and transfer to a 900 ml (1½ pint) ovenproof dish.

Whisk the egg whites until stiff. Add half the sugar, whisk again then fold in the remaining sugar with a metal spoon. Spread the meringue over the gooseberries to cover them completely. Bake in a preheated oven at 180°C (350°F), Gas Mark 4 for 15 minutes or until golden brown.

Serve hot, warm or cold.

Serves 4

Spicy Fruit Salad; Gooseberry Snow

GRAPEFRUIT SALAD

2 yellow grapefruit
1 pink grapefruit
250 g (8 oz) seedless white grapes
2 teaspoons creme de menthe (optional)
mint sprigs, to decorate

Peel the grapefruit. Holding the grapefruit over a serving bowl to catch the juice, separate the segments and remove all the pith, skin and pips. Cut the flesh into bite-sized pieces.

Add the grapes to the bowl, stirring lightly so that the different coloured fruits are evenly mixed. Sprinkle over the liqueur, if liked, and chill in the refrigerator for 1 hour before serving. Decorate with sprigs of mint.

Serves 4

PRUNE AND CHESTNUT MOUSSE

250 g (8 oz) dried prunes
25 g (1 oz) sugar
1 tablespoon lemon juice
125 g (4 oz) sweetened chestnut purée
142 ml (¼ pint) carton double cream
2 egg whites
crushed macaroons, to decorate

Soak the prunes in water overnight. Place in a small saucepan. Add the sugar and poach the prunes until they are soft. Remove the stones and purée the prunes in a blender or food processor with a little of the cooking liquid. Add the lemon juice and stir in the chestnut purée. Whip the cream until thick and fold it into the mixture. Beat the egg whites until they are stiff and fold in. Divide the mousse between 6 glass serving dishes and chill in the refrigerator. Decorate with crushed macaroons to serve.

Serves 6

SPICY ORANGE CREAMED RICE

25 g (1 oz) pudding rice
150 ml (¼ pint) water
300 ml (½ pint) milk
25 g (1 oz) soft brown sugar
1 teaspoon finely grated orange rind
¼ teaspoon grated nutmeg
1-2 tablespoons sultanas
1 bay leaf
15 g (½ oz) butter

Place the rice in a saucepan with the water. Bring to the boil, cover and simmer for 10 minutes. Drain and place the rice in a 600 ml (1 pint) ovenproof dish. Add the remaining ingredients.

Cook in a preheated moderate oven, 160°C (325°F), Gas Mark 3, for 1½ to 2 hours, stirring twice during the first hour to incorporate the skin and increase the creaminess. Serve hot or cold.

Serves 2

Spicy Orange Creamed Rice

ORANGE AND APRICOT MOUSSE

750 g (1½ lb) fresh apricots, stoned
150 g (5 oz) sugar
4 tablespoons water
grated rind and juice of 2 oranges
2 teaspoons agar-agar powder
142 ml (¼ pint) carton double cream
3 egg whites
grated chocolate to decorate

Place the apricots in a pan with the sugar and half the water. Cook gently until soft. Stir in the orange rind and juice. Purée in a blender and return to the pan. Add the agar-agar powder and boil for 2 minutes. Leave to cool.

Whisk the double cream until thick and fold into the purée. Beat the egg whites until they form stiff peaks and fold in. Divide the mousse between 4 individual serving dishes and chill before serving, decorated with a little grated chocolate.

Serves 4

BAKED APRICOTS

1 kg (2 lb) fresh ripe apricots
4-5 tablespoons caster sugar
142 ml (¼ pint) carton double cream
flaked almonds, to decorate

Wipe the apricots with kitchen towels. Cut them in half, remove the stones, and place in a single layer in a shallow ovenproof dish. Sprinkle the sugar on top, cover and leave overnight for the juice to run out.

Place the apricots in their juice, in the same dish, in a preheated oven, 180°C (350°F), Gas Mark 4 for 20 minutes until just soft. Allow to cool. Scatter flaked almonds on top and serve with whipped cream.

Serves 6

SUMMER FRUITS AND SOURED CREAM DESSERT

25 g (1 oz) sugar
4 tablespoons water
175 g (6 oz) red plums, stoned
125 g (4 oz) raspberries
4 tablespoons soured cream
2 teaspoons brown sugar

Place the sugar and water in a saucepan and heat gently until dissolved. Increase the heat and boil steadily for 2 minutes. Allow to cool, then chill.

Cut the plums into slices. Divide the plums and raspberries between individual serving dishes and pour over the syrup.

Spoon the soured cream over the fruit and sprinkle with brown sugar. Serve chilled.

Serves 2

Summer Fruits and Soured Cream Dessert

MACAROON PEACHES

3-4 tablespoons crushed macaroons
4 peaches or nectarines, halved and stoned
2 egg whites
125 g (4 oz) caster sugar
125 g (4 oz) ground almonds
25 g (1 oz) flaked almonds

Place the crushed macaroons in the bottom of an ovenproof dish that will hold the peach halves in a single layer. Place the halved fruit on top, cut side up. Whisk the egg whites until fluffy and sprinkle over 1 tablespoon of sugar. Continue whisking until the mixture stands in stiff peaks. Combine the remaining sugar with the ground almonds and fold into the meringue. Spoon over the peaches and scatter the flaked almonds on top. Bake in a preheated oven at 150°C (300°F), Gas Mark 2 for 30 minutes or until the meringue is pale gold. Serve immediately.
Serves 4

APPLE CHARLOTTE

750 g (1½ lb) cooking apples, peeled, cored and sliced
250 g (8 oz) caster sugar
1 egg, separated
150 g (5 oz) unsalted butter, melted
8 slices white bread, crusts removed, cut into fingers

Place the apples in a heavy saucepan with 175 g (6 oz) of the sugar and 1-2 tablespoons water. Heat gently, stirring from time to time. When the apple begins to soften, increase the heat and cook until the slices are reduced to a pulp. Remove from the heat, allow to cool slightly and beat in the egg yolk.

Brush the inside of a 1.2 litre (2 pint) souffle dish or cake tin with melted butter. Sprinkle 25 g (1 oz) of sugar over the butter. Dip both sides of the bread fingers into melted butter and use to line the dish completely, leaving enough bread to make a 'lid'. Brush the slices with lightly beaten egg white where they overlap.

Spoon the apple puree into the dish and cover with the remaining bread. Bake in a preheated oven at 190°C (375°F), Gas Mark 5 for 1 hour or until the crust is golden brown. Invert the charlotte on to a warmed serving dish and sprinkle the remaining sugar on top. Serve immediately. If you do not wish to serve the pudding straight away, keep it warm in the dish and turn it out when you are ready.
Serves 6

PREPARING APPLES

The flesh of apples turns brown very quickly after peeling if exposed to the air. To prevent this, have ready a bowl of lightly salted water to which you have added a teaspoon of vinegar or lemon juice, and drop the pieces of apple in as you work.

To freeze cooking apples, peel and slice, soak in water with lemon juice for 15 minutes. Pat dry on paper towels and open freeze on a tray before packing into bags.

HONEY-BAKED PEARS

8 firm pears, peeled
SYRUP
450 ml (¾ pint) water
½ teaspoon cloves
2 cinnamon sticks
3 tablespoons light soft brown sugar
6 tablespoons clear honey

Place the pears in an ovenproof dish which holds them snugly in an even layer. Place 450 ml (¾ pint) water in a saucepan. Add the cloves, cinnamon, sugar and honey and heat gently, stirring, until the sugar has melted. Bring the syrup slowly to the boil and strain over the pears. Bake in a preheated oven at 200°C (400°F). Gas Mark 6, or until the pears are tender, basting them occasionally. Serve hot, or leave the pears to cool in the syrup.
Serves 8

CHILLED PINEAPPLE CREAMS

2 eggs, separated
65 g (1½ oz) caster sugar
150 g (5 oz); mascarpone cheese
pinch of salt
1 × 432 g (14 oz) can crushed pineapple, drained

Beat the egg yolks with the sugar until pale and fluffy. Fold in the mascarpone a tablespoon a time until smoothly blended. Whisk the egg whites with a pinch of salt until they stand in stiff peaks. Fold into the mascarpone mixture using a metal spoon. Finally fold in the crushed pineapple a tablespoon at a time. Transfer the mixture into a dish and chill thoroughly in the refrigerator. To serve, spoon the creams into individual dishes.
Serves 6

SATSUMA FOOL

1 × 425 g (14 oz) can satsuma segments, drained
284 ml (½ pint) double cream
caster sugar, to taste
1 tablespoon orange liqueur (optional)
rind of 1 orange, to decorate

Purée the satsuma segments in a blender or food processor. Whip the cream until thick, add sugar to taste and orange liqueur if liked. Combine the cream with the fruit puree. Spoon into 4 individual dishes and serve chilled with a twist of orange rind on each one.
Serves 4

Honey-baked Pears; Chilled Pineapple Creams; Satsuma Fool

BLACKCURRANT FOOL

1 tablespoon custard powder
300 ml (½ pint) milk
1-2 tablespoons sugar
300 g (10 oz) blackcurrants
1 tablespoon water
sugar, to taste
150 g (5 oz) carton natural yogurt
few blackcurrants to decorate

Blend the custard powder with a little of the milk. Heat the remaining milk and stir into the custard mixture, then return to the pan. Heat, stirring continuously until the custard thickens. Cook for 1 minute. Add sugar to taste and leave to cool.

Place the blackcurrants in a pan with the water. Cook gently until the fruit is soft. Add sugar to taste and leave to cool. Place the fruit in a blender or pass through a sieve to make a purée.

Add the fruit purée and yogurt to the custard and whisk until well blended. Spoon into 4 individual serving dishes and decorate with blackcurrants. Chill before serving.
Serves 4

LEMON SYLLABUB

grated rind of 1 lemon
juice of 2 lemons
4 tablespoons medium or dry sherry
2 tablespoons brandy
125 g (4 oz) caster sugar
284 ml (½ pint) carton double cream
125 g (4 oz) fresh or frozen raspberries, sieved

Mix the lemon rind with the lemon juice, sherry, brandy and half the sugar. Chill for 30 minutes.

Meanwhile, whip the cream with the remaining sugar until it stands in soft peaks. Gradually whisk in the lemon mixture until thick and chill well.

To serve, place a small spoonful of the raspberry purée in the base of 4 serving glasses. Cover with the lemon syllabub then drop an even quantity of the remaining raspberry purée into the centre of each glass.

Serve chilled with sponge or shortbread fingers.
Serves 4

LEMON YOGURT SPARKLE

300 ml (½ pint) home-made or canned custard
300 g (10 oz) Greek-style yogurt
grated rind of 1 lemon
juice of 2 lemons
clear honey or sugar to taste
1 egg white

Mix the custard with the yogurt, lemon rind, lemon juice and honey or sugar to taste. Place in a freezerproof container and freeze until half frozen. whisking twice during this time to break down the ice crystals.

Whisk the egg white until it stands in stiff peaks. Fold into the semi-frozen mixture and freeze until firm.

Remove from the freezer about 10 to 15 minutes before using so that the lemon sparkle will soften sufficiently to scoop easily. Serve scooped into chilled glasses.
Serves 4 to 6

STRAWBERRY CHEESECAKE

BASE:
25 g (1 oz) butter
5 digestive biscuits, crushed

FILLING:
150 ml (¼ pint) water
2 teaspoons agar-agar powder
1 tablespoon lemon juice
grated rind of 1 lemon
250 g (8 oz) cottage cheese, sieved

TOPPING:
1½ teaspoons arrowroot
2 tablespoons lemon juice
6 tablespoons water
250 g (8 oz) strawberries, washed and hulled

Melt the butter and mix with the biscuit crumbs. Press into the base of a lightly greased 18 cm (7 inch) flan ring on a serving plate, or into a flan dish. Leave until firm.

To make the filling: heat the water in a pan and add the agar-agar. Boil until the agar is dissolved then leave to cool. Add the lemon juice, rind and cottage cheese. Mix well and pour over the biscuit base. Chill in the refrigerator until set. Remove the ring, if used.

To make the topping: blend the arrowroot with the lemon juice in a small pan, then stir in the water. Heat, stirring, until the mixture thickens and clears. Leave to cool a little.

Decorate the cheesecake with the strawberries and spoon the glaze over the top. Chill before serving.
Serves 6

FAMILY FRUIT SALAD

juice and grated rind of 1 lemon
2 red-skinned apples
2 bananas, peeled
1 × 213 g (7 oz) can peach slices
1 × 227 g (8 oz) can pineapple pieces
2 oranges

Pour the lemon juice into a glass serving dish. Core and slice the apples, slice the bananas, and add both to the dish. Add the peaches and pineapple with their syrup. Remove all the skin and pith from the oranges, cut into slices, and add to the fruit salad with any juice. Mix the fruits together thoroughly and sprinkle with the lemon rind. Chill for at least 1 hour before serving.
Serves 6

LEFT: *Blackcurrant Fool*

RIGHT: *Strawberry Cheesecake*

GREEK PINEAPPLE SURPRISE

1 large pineapple
50 g (2 oz) icing sugar, sifted
grated rind of ½ orange
3 tablespoons orange liqueur
125 g (4 oz) strawberries, sliced
125 g (4 oz) grapes, halved and deseeded
200 g (7 oz) Greek yogurt
caster sugar to taste

Halve the pineapple lengthways, scoop out the flesh and cut into cubes, discarding the central core. Reserve the shells.

Place the pineapple flesh in a bowl with the icing sugar and orange rind, pour over the liqueur and leave to soak for 2 hours.

Select a few strawberries and grapes for decoration and set aside. Fold the remaining strawberries and grapes into the Greek yogurt with the pineapple mixture. Add caster sugar to taste if desired.

Spoon into the reserved pineapple shells, decorate with the reserved fruit and chill for 30 minutes before serving.

Serves 4 to 6

AGAR-AGAR AND VEGETABLE GEL POWDERS

Agar-agar and vegetable gel powders are used by vegetarians instead of gelatine, which is of animal origin. Agar-agar is made from edible seaweed. To set 600 ml (1 pint) of liquid, whisk it with 2 tsp powdered agar-agar and bring to the boil stirring. Simmer for 5 minutes.

Alternatively, mix 2 teaspoons vegetable gel powder with a little cold water then added to about 600 ml (1 pint) of the cold liquid to be set. The mixture then needs to be boiled for 2 minutes.

BAKED APPLES

4 cooking apples
1 teaspoon ground cinnamon
25 g (1 oz) butter
25 g (1 oz) icing sugar, sifted
1 egg yolk
50 g (2 oz) ground almonds
grated rind of 1 orange
25 g (1 oz) demerara sugar
4 tablespoons water

Core the apples, then make a cut in the skin around the middle. Stand them in an ovenproof dish and sprinkle cinnamon around the inside of the core cavities.

Cream together the butter, icing sugar, egg yolk, almonds and orange rind and spoon into the apples. Top with demerara sugar.

Pour the water into the dish, then bake in a preheated moderate oven, 180°C (350°F), Gas Mark 4, for 45 minutes to 1 hour, until the apples are tender.

Serves 4

GINGER LAYER DESSERT

3 × 213 g (7 oz) cans peach slices, mandarins or pear quarters, or a mixture of these
1 × 200 g (7 oz) packet gingersnaps, broken into pieces
284 ml (½ pint) carton double cream, lightly whipped
chocolate vermicelli to decorate

Drain the cans of fruit, reserving the syrup. Place one third of the gingersnaps in a layer in the bottom of a 1.2 litre (2 pint) soufflé dish and spoon over just enough of the fruit syrup to moisten the biscuits. Arrange one third of the fruit on top and cover with a layer of cream.

Repeat the layers twice and chill in the refrigerator for a few hours. Decorate with chocolate vermicelli before serving.

Serves 4 to 6

PEARS WITH CHOCOLATE SAUCE

8 peeled fresh, or canned pear halves
125 g (4 oz) plain chocolate, chopped
15 g (½ oz) butter
2 tablespoons golden syrup
2 tablespoons milk
TOPPING:
whipped cream
chopped walnuts (optional)

Arrange the pear halves in 4 individual serving dishes. Place the chocolate in a basin over a pan of boiling water and add the butter and syrup. When melted stir in the milk. Pour the sauce over the pears, allow to cool, then top with cream. Sprinkle with chopped walnuts, if liked

Serves 4

BAKED GOOSEBERRY SPONGE

75 g (3 oz) unsalted butter, melted
4 tablespoons demerara sugar
750 g (1½ lb) gooseberries, topped and tailed
SPONGE MIXTURE
1 egg
1 egg yolk
175 g (6 oz) granulated sugar
100 g (3½ oz) plain flour, sifted
125 g (4 oz) unsalted butter, melted

Pour the melted butter into a 1.2 litre (2 pint) ovenproof dish and stir in the demerara sugar. Place the gooseberries on top.

Make the sponge mixture. In a mixing bowl whisk together the egg, egg yolk and sugar until thick and foamy. Fold in the flour. Pour the butter down the side of the bowl then fold it in. Pour this mixture over the gooseberries.

Bake in a preheated oven at 180°C (350°F), Gas Mark 4 for about 1 hour or until the top is golden brown. Serve warm with vanilla ice cream.

Serves 6

Ginger Layer Dessert; Pears with Chocolate Sauce; Baked Gooseberry Sponge

RICH CHOCOLATE SAUCE

4 sugar lumps
1 orange
75 g (3 oz) granulated sugar
300 ml (½ pint) water
175 g (6 oz) plain chocolate, in pieces

Rub the lumps of sugar over the orange rind to soak up the flavour and colour. Place in a pan with the granulated sugar and water and heat gently, stirring, until the sugar is dissolved. Bring to the boil and boil for 5 minutes without stirring. Remove from the heat.

Add the chocolate, stir until melted, then beat well. Return to the heat and simmer until the sauce is syrupy. Serve cold with ice cream or profiteroles, or heat gently, stirring, to serve with puddings.

Makes about 450 ml (¾ pint)

BUTTERSCOTCH SAUCE

1 tablespoon cornflour
150 ml (¼ pint) milk
25 g (1 oz) butter
125 g (4 oz) light soft brown sugar
½ teaspoon vanilla essence

Mix the cornflour to a smooth paste with a little of the milk. Heat the remaining milk in a pan with the butter and sugar until dissolved and melted. Stir the cornflour mixture into the milk and cook, stirring constantly, until the sauce comes to the boil and thickens. Add the vanilla essence and simmer for 3 to 5 minutes.

Serve hot with steamed and baked puddings, over sliced bananas or as an ice cream topping.

Serves 4 to 6

STRAWBERRY AND BRANDY SAUCE

6 tablespoons strawberry jam
grated rind and juice of ½ lemon
2 tablespoons plum or fruit brandy

Place the jam in a small pan and heat gently until bubbling. Add the lemon rind, lemon juice and brandy, mixing well.

Serve warm with ice cream.

Serves 4

RASPBERRY SAUCE

250 g (8 oz) raspberries
25 g (1 oz) caster sugar
3 tablespoons white wine

Place all the ingredients in a food processor and blend until smooth.

Serve warm or cold with fresh or grilled peaches or ice cream.

Makes 300 ml (½ pint)

LEFT: *Rich Chocolate Sauce; Butterscotch Sauce*
RIGHT: *Raspberry Sauce; Raspberry and Redcurrant Sauce; St Clements Marmalade Sauce*

RASPBERRY AND REDCURRANT SAUCE

500 g (1 lb) redcurrants
2 tablespoons water
125 g (4 oz) caster sugar
500 g (1 lb) raspberries

Put the redcurrants in a pan with the water and sugar. Heat gently until the sugar is dissolved, then simmer until the fruit is soft. Add the raspberries and leave until cool.

Purée the fruit mixture in a blender then strain, or rub through a sieve. Serve cold with ice cream, or heat gently to serve with puddings.

Makes about 900 ml (1½ pints)

ST CLEMENTS MARMALADE SAUCE

2 teaspoons arrowroot or cornflour
150 ml (¼ pint) cold water
4 tablespoons orange marmalade
2 teaspoons lemon juice
1 teaspoon grated lemon rind
1 tablespoon caster sugar

Mix the arrowroot or cornflour to a smooth paste with a little of the cold water. Place the remaining water in a pan with the marmalade, lemon juice, lemon rind and sugar. Heat gently, stirring constantly, until the sugar has dissolved.

Remove the pan from the heat, stir in the arrowroot or cornflour mixture, mixing well. Return to the heat, bring to the boil and cook until the sauce is clear and thickened. Simmer for 2 minutes.

Serve hot with baked or steamed sponge or suet puddings.

Serves 4 to 6

BAKING

Sweet-toothed or savoury, here are a selection of time-honoured baked favourites that make meals from breakfast to supper something really special. Here you'll find the veritable baker's dozen (and more) recipes for large and small cakes, breads and rolls, savoury and sweet pastries, pies and crisp biscuits and cookies.

If you enjoy the warmth and nourishment provided by home-baked breads then you'll find the recipes for Wholemeal Bread, Soda Bread, Herb Bread and Sesame Baps good never-fail favourites. If you like the comforting sizzling and hissing sound of baked fare on the griddle then you'll enjoy making Pikelets. If you batch-bake regularly for the biscuit tin or cookie jar then the recipes for Cheese and Peanut Biscuits, Cocoa Biscuits and Meringues won't go amiss. But if it's sweet-toothed cakes and pastries on which you stake your teatime reputation then don't waste a minute in turning to the recipes for Lemon Vanilla Buns, Royal Raisin Squares, Cinnamon Crumble Cake, Figgy Prune Cake and Muscatel Cake.

LEMON VANILLA BUNS

250 g (8 oz) butter
75 g (3 oz) vanilla sugar (see note)
2-3 drops vanilla essence
75 g (3 oz) cornflour
75 g (3 oz) plain flour, sifted
TO FINISH:
icing sugar, sifted
lemon curd

In a mixing bowl beat the butter with the vanilla sugar until light and soft. Add the vanilla essence. Sift the two flours over the mixture and fold in until blended. Divide the mixture evenly between 12 paper cases in a bun tin. Use a teaspoon to swirl a circular pattern on each bun.

Bake in a preheated oven at 180°C (350°F), Gas Mark 4 for 20 minutes until risen and light gold in colour. Allow to cool on a wire rack.

Sift icing sugar on top and place a teaspoonful of lemon curd in the centre of each bun.

Makes 12

SWEET AND SPICY TARTS

175 g (6 oz) shortcrust pastry (see Spinach Cheese Flan, page 91)
250 g (8 oz) golden syrup
1 tablespoon rum or brandy
50 g (2 oz) fresh white breadcrumbs
1 teaspoon ground cinnamon or ground ginger
1 teaspoon lemon juice

Roll out the pastry on a floured surface. Cut out 12 rounds with a 8 cm (3 inch) fancy pastry cutter and place them in a bun tin. Reroll the pastry trimmings and cut into strips.

Gently heat the syrup with the rum in a small heavy-bottomed saucepan. Combine the breadcrumbs with the spice and stir into the syrup. Add the lemon juice. Divide the mixture evenly between the cases and decorate with pastry strips. Bake in a preheated oven at 200°C (400°F), Gas Mark 6 for 10-15 minutes.

Makes 12

DANISH PASTRIES

15 g (½ oz) dried yeast
150 ml (¼ pint) warm milk
500 g (1 lb) plain flour
300 g (10 oz) butter
50 g (2 oz) caster sugar
2 eggs
FILLING:
50 g (2 oz) butter
50 g (2 oz) caster sugar
50 g (2 oz) currants
2 teaspoons mixed spice
TO FINISH:
250 g (8 oz) icing sugar, sifted
2 tablespoons water

Soak the yeast in the milk for 10 minutes. Put the flour, 50 g (2 oz) butter and the sugar in a food processor. Beat the eggs with the milk and yeast and pour in through the feed tube. Process for 1 minute. Roll out on a floured surface to an oblong 28 × 18 cm (11 × 7 inches). Put remaining butter, in a block, in the centre. Fold over top and bottom edges, give a quarter turn and roll out. Repeat turning and rolling 4 times. Cover and chill for 1 hour.

Meanwhile, place the butter and sugar in the bowl and process until smooth. Add the currants and spice and process for 5 seconds.

Roll out the dough to 40 × 25 cm (16 × 10 inches) and spread with the filling to within 1 cm (½ inch) of the edges. Roll up from a long edge and cut into 12 slices. Place on a greased baking sheet and leave to rise in a warm place for 20 minutes. Bake in a preheated hot oven, 220°C (425°F), Gas Mark 7, for 15 minutes. Cool.

Mix the icing sugar with the water. Spoon over each pastry while warm.

Makes 12

WALNUT MUFFINS

175 g (6 oz) self-raising flour
1 teaspoon salt
75 g (3 oz) walnut pieces, chopped
5 tablespoons golden syrup
5 tablespoons water
40 g (1½ oz) butter
1 egg, beaten

Sift the flour and salt into a bowl and stir in the walnuts. Make a well in the centre.

Place the syrup, water and butter in a pan and heat gently, stirring until the butter has melted. Pour into the well in the flour mixture and beat thoroughly. Beat in the egg to give a smooth batter.

Line a 12-hole bun tin with paper cases. Spoon in the batter to two-thirds fill the cases. Bake in a preheated moderately hot oven, 190°C (375°F), Gas Mark 5, for 20 minutes, until risen and firm to touch. Transfer to a wire rack to cool slightly.

Serve warm, split and buttered.

Makes 12

COCOA BISCUITS

125 g (4 oz) butter
50 g (2 oz) caster sugar
150 g (5 oz) plain flour
1 tablespoon cocoa

Cream together the fat and sugar, then sift and stir in the flour and cocoa. Roll the mixture into small balls and place well apart on greased baking sheets. Flatten the balls slightly.

Bake in a preheated moderate oven, 160°C (325°F), Gas Mark 3, for 30 minutes. Leave on the baking sheets for a few minutes, then transfer to a wire rack to cool.

Makes about 20

ROYAL RAISIN SQUARES

275 g (9 oz) plain or wholemeal shortcrust pastry (see Spinach Cheese Flan, page 91)

FILLING:
50 g (2 oz) cake crumbs
175 g (6 oz) raisins
1 egg yolk
1 teaspoon finely grated lemon rind

TOPPING:
250 g (8 oz) icing sugar
1 egg white
1 teaspoon lemon juice
3 tablespoons redcurrant jelly

Roll out the pastry on a floured surface and use to line the base of a 20 cm (8 inch) square cake tin. Put the filling ingredients in a food processor and process until blended. Spread over the pastry.

Place the icing sugar, egg white and lemon juice in a food processor and process until smooth. Pour over the filling.

Work the redcurrant jelly to a piping consistency in a bowl and spoon into a small piping bag fitted with a plain nozzle. Pipe a trellis design over the top of the cake.

Bake in a preheated moderately hot oven, 190°C (375°F), Gas Mark 5, for 30 minutes, then lower the temperature to 180°C (350°F), Gas Mark 4, and bake for 10 minutes. Cool on a wire rack. Cut into squares when cold.

Makes 16

LEFT: *Sweet and Spicy Tarts; Danish Pastries; Lemon Vanilla Buns*

RIGHT: *Royal Raisin Squares*

VICTORIA SANDWICH

CAKE MIXTURE:
125 g (4 oz) butter, softened
125 g (4 oz) caster sugar
2 eggs
125 g (4 oz) self-raising flour
1 teaspoon baking powder
FILLING AND TOPPING:
jam or buttercream icing (see Butterfly Cakes opposite)
crystallized orange or lemon slices to decorate (optional)

Place all the cake ingredients in a bowl and beat thoroughly for 2 minutes until smooth, using an electric beater if possible.

Divide the mixture between two lined and greased 18 cm (7 inch) sandwich tins and bake in a preheated moderate oven, 160°C (325°F), Gas Mark 3, for 30 to 35 minutes until the cakes are golden and springy to the touch. Turn out and cool on a wire rack.

Sandwich together with jam or buttercream icing. Spread more icing over the top and decorate with orange slices if liked.

Makes one 18 cm (7 inch) cake

VARIATIONS: Any of the following can be added to the basic ingredients: few drops of vanilla or almond essence;
1 tablespoon cocoa dissolved in 2 tablespoons hot water;
2 teaspoons instant coffee dissolved in 1 tablespoon hot water.

BUTTERFLY CAKES

1 quantity Victoria Sandwich mixture, plain, chocolate or coffee-flavoured (see opposite)
BUTTERCREAM ICING:
75 g (3 oz) butter, softened
175 g (6 oz) icing sugar, sifted
1-2 tablespoons warm water
flavouring (see note)
TO DECORATE:
icing sugar, sifted

Divide the mixture between about 20 greased bun tins.

Bake in a preheated moderately hot oven, 190°C (375°F), Gas Mark 5, for about 15 minutes until golden brown and firm. Transfer to a wire rack to cool.

To make the icing, beat together the butter, icing sugar and warm water until well mixed. Stir in the flavouring.

Cut a slice off the top of each cake and pipe or spoon in a little icing. Cut the slices in half and replace on the cakes to resemble butterfly wings. Sprinkle with icing sugar.

Makes about 20

NOTE: Flavour the icing with any of the following:
1 tablespoon cocoa dissolved in a little hot water;
2 teaspoons instant coffee dissolved in a little hot water

PIKELETS

2 teaspoons dried yeast
1 teaspoon caster sugar
250 ml (8 fl oz) warm milk
250 g (8 oz) plain flour
1 teaspoon salt
2 eggs

Sprinkle the yeast and sugar into the milk and set aside until just beginning to froth. Whisk lightly.

Sift the flour and salt into a mixing bowl and make a well in the centre. Add the eggs and half the milk mixture and, using a wooden spoon, gradually mix to a smooth, thick consistency. Stir in the remaining milk, cover and set aside in a warm place for about 30 minutes.

Meanwhile, heat a griddle or heavy-based frying pan until very hot; grease well.

Stir the batter lightly and pour enough onto the griddle or pan to make a 13-15 cm (5-6 inch) pikelet; the batter will spread and it will look like a thick pancake. When the surface begins to bubble and the edges are tinged golden brown, turn with a palette knife and cook the other side until lightly browned. Keep hot as for pancakes or crêpes.

Spread liberally with butter and serve immediately.

Makes 8 to 10

LEFT: *Victoria Sandwich; Butterfly Cakes*

RIGHT: *Teatime Scones*

TEATIME SCONES

250 g (8 oz) self-raising flour
½ teaspoon baking powder
50 g (2 oz) butter
2 tablespoons caster sugar
150 ml (¼ pint) milk (approximately)

Sift the flour and baking powder into a bowl. Rub in the fat until the mixture resembles breadcrumbs, then stir in the sugar. Add enough milk to give a fairly soft dough.

Turn onto a lightly floured surface, knead very gently then roll out to a 2 cm (¾ inch) thickness. Cut into 5 cm (2 inch) rounds and place on a lightly floured baking sheet. Brush with milk and bake in a preheated hot oven, 220°C (425°F), Gas Mark 7, for 10 minutes. Cool on a wire rack.

Cut in half and spread with butter and jam to serve.

Makes 10 to 12

COFFEE AND CREAM CAKE

175 g (6 oz) caster sugar
175 g (6 oz) soft margarine
3 eggs
175 g (6 oz) self raising flour
2 tablespoons strong black coffee
FILLING:
125 g (4 oz) unsalted butter
250 g (8 oz) icing sugar, sifted
2-3 drops vanilla essence
TO DECORATE
grated chocolate

Place all the cake ingredients in a mixing bowl or food processor and beat or process until light and fluffy. Divide the mixture evenly between two lined and greased 20 cm (8 inch) sandwich tins and smooth the tops. Bake in a preheated oven at 160°C (325°F) Gas Mark 3 for 35 minutes until golden in colour and firm to the touch. Turn on to a wire rack, remove the lining paper and leave the cakes to cool.

To make the filling, place all the ingredients in a bowl and mix together thoroughly until light and fluffy. Use half the butter icing to sandwich the two cakes together. Spread the remainder evenly over the top and make a pattern with the blade of a palette knife. Sprinkle a border of grated choclate on top and transfer to a serving dish.

Serves 6–8

MERINGUES

2 egg whites (size 1-2)
125 g (4 oz) caster sugar
175 ml (6 fl oz) double cream, whipped with 1 tablespoon caster sugar

Put the egg whites in a large mixing bowl and whisk until stiff. Whisk in 2 tablespoons of the sugar. Fold in the remaining sugar with a metal spoon.

Put the mixture into a piping bag fitted with 1 cm (½ inch) plain nozzle and pipe 16 rounds on a baking sheet lined with oiled greaseproof paper or non-stick baking parchment.

Bake in a very cool oven, 120°C (225°F), Gas Mark ¼, for about 3 hours or until the meringues are firm to the touch. Leave on the baking sheet until completely cold.

Sandwich the meringues together in pairs with cream just before serving.

Makes 8

SPICY HONEY AND OAT COOKIES

125 g (4 oz) butter
5 tablespoons clear honey
125 g (4 oz) light soft brown sugar
175 g (6 oz) self-raising flour, sifted
125 g (4 oz) porridge oats
50 g (2 oz) currants
1 teaspoon ground ginger

Melt the butter with the honey in a pan over a low heat. Stir in the sugar, flour, porridge oats, currants and ginger until well mixed.

Divide the mixture into 16 pieces and shape into small balls. Press lightly onto greased baking sheets, making sure they are well apart.

Bake in a preheated moderate oven, 180°C (350°F), Gas Mark 4, for about 15 minutes or until lightly browned and firm to the touch.

Cool slightly on the baking sheets, then transfer to a wire rack to cool completely.

Makes 16

LEFT: *Coffee and Cream Cake*

RIGHT: *Moist Fruit Cake; Chocolate Bars*

MOIST FRUIT CAKE

175 g (6 oz) raisins
175 g (6 oz) sultanas
175 g (6 oz) currants
250 g (8 oz) soft brown sugar
½ teaspoon ground cinnamon
½ teaspoon ground ginger
175 g (6 oz) butter
250 ml (8 fl oz) water
3 eggs, beaten
150 g (5 oz) plain flour
150 g (5 oz) self-raising flour
½ teaspoon bicarbonate of soda
50 g (2 oz) glacé cherries, chopped
50 g (2 oz) mixed peel
50 g (2 oz) walnuts, chopped

Put the raisins, sultanas, currants, sugar, spices and butter into a saucepan with the water. Bring to the boil, stirring. Simmer for 3 minutes then leave to cool. When cold, stir in the eggs.

Sift the flours and bicarbonate of soda into a mixing bowl and stir in the cherries, peel and nuts. Stir in the fruit and egg mixture until thoroughly mixed, then turn into a lined and greased 23 cm (9 inch) round cake tin.

Bake in a preheated moderate oven, 160°C (325°F), Gas Mark 3, for 1½ to 1¾ hours. Turn out and cool on a wire rack.

Makes one 23 cm (9 inch) cake

CHOCOLATE BARS

175 g (6 oz) wholemeal flour
75 g (3 oz) muesli
½ teaspoon bicarbonate of soda
25 g (1 oz) glace cherries, chopped
175 g (6 oz) butter
175 g (6 oz) dark brown soft sugar
200 g (7 oz) plain chocolate

Combine the flour, muesli, bicarbonate of soda and cherries in a mixing bowl. Rub in the butter with the fingertips. Stir in the sugar. Spoon the mixture into a greased 28 × 18 cm (11 × 7 inch) Swiss roll tin and spread to an even layer. Bake in a preheated oven at 160°C (325°F), Gas Mark 3 for 30 minutes. Leave to cool in the tin. Melt the chocolate, pour it over the cake and leave to set. Cut into squares when cool.

Makes 20

CINNAMON CRUMBLE CAKE

125 g (4 oz) butter, softened
125 g (4 oz) soft brown sugar
2 eggs
50 g (2 oz) ground rice
125 g (4 oz) plain flour
1½ teaspoons baking powder
CRUMBLE:
50 g (2 oz) soft brown sugar
1 teaspoon cinnamon

Put the butter and sugar in a food processor and process until pale.

Add the eggs one at a time with the machine switched on. Switch off the machine. Add the dry ingredients to the bowl through the feed tube and process for a few seconds to blend.

Turn into a greased 20 cm (8 inch) loose-bottomed cake tin and smooth the surface. Mix the crumble ingredients and sprinkle over the top.

Bake in a preheated moderate oven, 180°C (350°F), Gas Mark 4, for 35 to 45 minutes, until a skewer inserted into the centre comes out clean.

Leave in the tin until cold, then carefully push out and slide onto a serving plate.

Makes one 20 cm (8 inch) cake

BANANA CAKE

125 g (4 oz) butter, softened
175 g (6 oz) caster sugar
2 eggs
250 g (8 oz) self-raising flour
2 ripe bananas, roughly chopped
TO FINISH:
4 tablespoons lemon curd
2 firm bananas, sliced
3 tablespoons lemon juice
125 g (4 oz) icing sugar, sifted

Put all the cake ingredients in a food processor and process until smooth.

Divide between 2 lined and greased 18 cm (7 inch) sandwich tins and bake in a preheated moderate oven, 180°C (350°F), Gas Mark 4, for 25 to 30 minutes. Turn onto a wire rack to cool.

Sandwich the cake together with the lemon curd and half of the banana slices. Sprinkle the remaining banana with 1 tablespoon lemon juice. Warm the remaining 2 tablespoons lemon juice and gradually mix into the icing sugar to make a smooth coating icing. Spread over the top of the cake and decorate with the banana slices.

Makes one 18 cm (7 inch) cake

UPSIDE DOWN CAKE

125 (4 oz) butter
125 g (4 oz) soft brown sugar
2 eggs
125 g (4 oz) self-raising flour
TOPPING:
75 g (3 oz) butter
75 g (3 oz) soft brown sugar
1 × 432 g (15 oz) can pineapple slices
4 glacé cherries, halved

First prepare the topping. Put the butter and sugar in a food processor and process until pale. Spread over the base of a 20 cm (8 inch) cake tin. Drain the pineapple slices, reserving the syrup, and arrange on top. Place a cherry half in each ring.

Place the cake ingredients in the processor bowl, adding 2 tablespoons of the pineapple juice, and process until smooth. Spoon the mixture over the pineapple and bake in a preheated moderate oven, 180°C (350°F), Gas Mark 4, for 45 minutes, until firm. Transfer to a wire rack.

Serve warm or cold.

Makes one 20 cm (8 inch) cake

LEFT: *Cinnamon Crumble Cake; Banana Cake; Upside Down Cake*

RIGHT: *Carrot Pistachio Cake; Muscatel Cake*

CARROT PISTACHIO CAKE

2 eggs
1 teaspoon ground cardamom
125 g (4 oz) caster sugar
125 g (4 oz) butter, softened
250 g (8 oz) plain flour
1 teaspoon bicarbonate of soda
250 g (8 oz) carrots, finely grated
50 g (2 oz) Pistachio nuts, chopped
50 g (2 oz) ground almonds
125 g (4 oz) raisins

Put the eggs, cardamom, sugar and butter in a food processor and process until smooth. Add the flour and bicarbonate of soda down the feed tube and process for 5 seconds. Add the remaining ingredients and process for 5 seconds or until well mixed.

Turn into a well greased 23 cm (9 inch) cake tin and bake in a preheated moderate oven, 180°C (350°F), Gas Mark 4, for 40 minutes. Transfer to a wire rack to cool.

Makes one 23 cm (9 inch) cake

MUSCATEL CAKE

175 g (6 oz) butter, softened
175 g (6 oz) caster sugar
3 eggs
250 g (8 oz) plain flour
2 teaspoons baking powder
1½ tablespoons muscat wine
1 slice candied peel

Put all the ingredients, except the peel, in a food processor and process until combined and smooth.

Transfer to a greased 15 to 18 cm (6 to 7 inch) cake tin and place the slice of candied peel on top. Bake in a preheated moderate oven, 180°C (350°F), Gas Mark 4, for 1¼ hours. Leave in the tin for a few minutes, then turn onto a wire rack to cool.

Makes one 15 to 18 cm (6 to 7 inch) cake

NOTE: This is a Madeira-type case, which keeps well. Madeira or marsala wine, or sweet sherry could be used instead of muscat wine.

APRICOT AND NUT TEABREAD

125 g (4 oz) high-fibre bran
50 g (2 oz) muscovado sugar
75 g (3 oz) dried apricots, snipped
300 ml (½ pint) apple juice
125 g (4 oz) wholemeal flour
2 teaspoons baking powder, sifted
50 g (2 oz) hazelnuts, chopped

Place the High Fibre Bran, sugar, apricots and apple juice in a mixing bowl and leave to soak for 1 hour.

Stir the flour, baking powder and all but 1 tablespoon of the chopped hazelnuts into the apricot mixture and beat thoroughly.

Turn into a lined and greased 500 g (1 lb) loaf tin. Sprinkle the remaining nuts over the top and bake in a preheated moderate oven, 180°C (350°F), Gas Mark 4, for 55 to 60 minutes.

Turn onto a wire rack to cool. Cut into slices to serve.

Makes one 500 g (1 lb) loaf

FRUITED GINGERCAKE

125 g (4 oz) butter, softened
175 g (6 oz) light soft brown sugar
1 egg
1 tablespoon black treacle
2 × 185 g (7 oz) jars cranberry sauce
grated rind of 1 orange
50 g (2 oz) crystallized ginger, chopped
250 g (8 oz) self-raising flour
2 teaspoons ground ginger

Grease and line the base of a 20 cm (8 inch) deep round cake tin.

Beat the butter with the sugar until light and fluffy. Add the egg, treacle, cranberry sauce, orange rind and ginger pieces.

Sift the flour and ginger together and stir into the mixture until well blended. Spoon into the prepared cake tin and level the surface.

Bake in a preheated moderate oven, 180°C (350°F), Gas Mark 4, for about 1¼ to 1½ hours, until well risen, browned and a skewer pierced into the centre comes out clean. Cool on a wire rack.

Makes one 20 cm (8 inch) round cake

CRANBERRY NUT LOAF

250 g (8 oz) plain flour
1½ teaspoons baking powder
½ teaspoon bicarbonate of soda
1 teaspoon salt
50 g (2 oz) butter
125 g (4 oz) caster sugar
75 g (3 oz) chopped walnuts
grated rind and juice of 2 oranges
1 egg
1 × 185 g (7 oz) jar cranberry sauce

Grease and line the base of a 20 × 10 cm (8 × 4 inches) loaf tin.

Sift the flour with the baking powder, bicarbonate of soda and salt. Rub in the butter until the mixture resembles fine breadcrumbs. Stir in the sugar and walnuts.

Whisk together the orange rind and juice with the egg and cranberry sauce. Stir into the dry ingredients, mixing well. Spoon into the prepared tin.

Bake in a preheated oven, 180°C (350°F), Gas Mark 4, for about 1 hour until risen, browned and a skewer pierced into the centre comes out clean. Turn out and leave to cool on a wire rack.

Makes 1 loaf

Apricot and Nut Teabread

FIGGY PRUNE CAKE

125 g (4 oz) pitted prunes, chopped
125 g (4 oz) dried figs, chopped
150 ml (¼ pint) apple juice
75 g (3 oz) clear honey
125 ml (4 fl oz) corn oil
2 eggs, beaten
150 g (5 oz) wholemeal flour
½ teaspoon bicarbonate of soda
1 teaspoon ground mixed spice
½ teaspoon ground nutmeg
125 g (4 oz) natural yogurt
25 g (1 oz) walnuts chopped

Place the prunes and figs in a pan with the apple juice, cover and simmer gently for 10 minutes. Leave to cool. Stir in the remaining ingredients, except the walnuts, and mix thoroughly.

Pour into a lined and greased deep 20 cm (8 inch) cake tin and sprinkle the walnuts over the top. Bake in a preheated moderate oven, 180°C (350°F), Gas Mark 4, for 50 to 55 minutes, until firm to the touch. Leave in the tin for 2 minutes, then turn onto a wire rack to cool.

Makes one 20 cm (8 inch) cake

BEST-EVER BARM BRACK

125 g (4 oz) raisins
125 g (4 oz) sultanas
75 g (3 oz) currants
25 g (1 oz) chopped mixed peel
200 g (7 oz) soft brown sugar
450 ml (¾ pint) cold tea
275 g (9 oz) self-raising wholemeal flour, sifted
1 egg, beaten
2 tablespoons clear honey, warmed

Place the raisins, sultanas, currants, peel, sugar and tea in a large bowl. Cover and leave to soak overnight.

Add the flour and egg and mix well to blend. Spoon into a greased 500 g (1 lb) loaf tin, levelling the surface.

Bake in a preheated moderate oven, 180°C (350°F), Gas Mark 4, for 1½ to 1¾ hours.

While still hot, brush the top of the loaf with the warmed honey. Transfer to a wire rack to cool.

Serve cold, sliced and buttered if liked.

Makes one 500 g (1 lb) loaf

MALT LOAF

250 g (8 oz) self-raising flour
25 g (1 oz) butter
25 g (1 oz) soft brown sugar
150 ml (¼ pint) milk
2 teaspoons black treacle
1 rounded tablespoon malt extract
50 g (2 oz) sultanas
GLAZE:
1 tablespoon sugar
2 tablespoons water

Put the flour, butter and sugar in a food processor

Warm the milk, treacle and malt extract, pour down the feed tube and process until smooth. Add the sultanas and process for 2 seconds.

Turn into a well greased 500 g (1 lb) loaf tin and bake in a preheated moderate oven, 160°C (325°F), Gas Mark 3, for 1 hour, until golden. Turn onto a wire rack.

Boil the sugar and water together and use to brush the top of the loaf immediately. Leave until cold, preferably until the next day. Serve sliced and buttered.

Makes one 500 g (1 lb) loaf

Figgy Prune Cake

CRUNCHY WHOLEMEAL BREAD

125 g (4 oz) butter
50 g (2 oz) soft brown sugar
2 tablespoons black treacle
1 egg, beaten
125 g (4 oz) strong white plain flour
1 teaspoon each bicarbonate of soda and baking powder
125 g (4 oz) wholemeal flour
good pinch of salt
2 × 150 g (5 oz) cartons natural yogurt
175 g (6 oz) muesli

Cream the butter and sugar together until light and fluffy. Gradually beat in the treacle and egg.

Sift the plain flour, bicarbonate of soda and baking powder together into a bowl, then stir in the wholemeal flour and salt.

Gradually fold the flour mixture and yogurt alternately into the creamed mixture. Fold in the muesli.

Turn into a greased 1 kg (2 lb) loaf tin and smooth the top. Bake in a preheated moderate oven, 180°C (350°F), Gas Mark 4, for 1 hour, until well risen and golden brown. Cool on a wire rack.

Serve sliced and buttered.

Makes one 1 kg (2 lb) loaf

CHEESE AND PEANUT BISCUITS

50 g (2 oz) self-raising flour
½ teaspoon baking powder
¼ teaspoon salt
50 g (2 oz) wholemeal flour
25 g (1 oz) butter
25 g (1 oz) crunchy peanut butter
75 g (3 oz) Cheddar cheese, grated
25 g (1 oz) salted peanuts, finely chopped
1 large egg (size 1–2), beaten

Sift the self-raising flour, baking powder and salt into a bowl. Stir in the wholemeal flour. Rub in the butter and peanut butter until the mixture resembles fine breadcrumbs. Stir in the cheese and peanuts. Bind the mixture together with the egg.

Turn onto a lightly floured surface and knead until smooth. Roll out to a 5 mm (¼ inch) thickness and cut out rounds, using a 5 cm (2 inch) biscuit cutter. Place, well apart, on greased baking sheets.

Bake in a preheated moderately hot oven, 190°C (375°F), Gas Mark 5, for 10 to 15 minutes until lightly browned. Cool on a wire rack.

Makes about 25

CHEESE AND ONION PLAIT

500 g (1 lb) strong white plain flour
2 teaspoons salt
25 g (1 oz) butter
2 teaspoons dried yeast
1 teaspoon caster sugar
scant 300 ml (½ pint) lukewarm milk
1 egg, beaten

FILLING:

1 tablespoon oil
2 large onions, chopped
125 g (4 oz) matured Cheddar cheese, grated

TO FINISH:

beaten egg
25 g (1 oz) flaked almonds (optional)
pinch of salt (optional)

Sift the flour and salt into a bowl and rub in the butter until the mixture resembles fine breadcrumbs.

Combine the yeast, sugar and warm milk and leave in a warm place for about 10 minutes.

Add the yeast mixture and beaten egg to the flour and mix to a smooth dough. Turn onto a floured surface and knead for about 10 minutes, until the dough is smooth and not sticky. Cover and leave to rise in a warm place for about 1¼ hours, or until doubled in size.

Meanwhile, heat the oil in a pan, add the onions and fry until golden brown; leave to cool.

Knock back the dough and mix in the fried onions and grated cheese, making sure they are evenly distributed. Divide the dough in half, then divide each half into 3 equal portions. Roll each portion with the hands into 30-36 cm (12-14 inch) long ropes. Plait 3 pieces together and pinch the ends to secure. Repeat with the other 3 pieces.

Place each loaf on a baking sheet, cover with a plastic bag and leave in a warm place to rise for about 40 to 45 minutes.

Brush with beaten egg and bake in a preheated moderately hot oven, 200°C (400°F), Gas Mark 6, for 20 minutes. Brush again with egg and sprinkle with the almonds and salt, if using. Return to the oven for 20 to 25 minutes, until well risen and golden brown.

Cool on a wire rack. Serve with butter, and cheese if liked.

Makes 2 plaits

Crunchy Wholemeal Bread; Cheese and Onion Plait

SODA BREAD

500 g (1 lb) wholemeal flour
250 g (8 oz) plain flour
1 teaspoon sugar
1 teaspoon salt
2 teaspoons bicarbonate of soda
500 ml (18 fl oz) buttermilk
2 tablespoons milk to glaze

Sift the dry ingredients into a bowl. Make a well in the centre and pour in the buttermilk. Stir the flour in from the side and knead lightly until smooth. Divide the dough in half and shape into 2 rounds.

Place on a greased baking sheet and mark each round into quarters, using a sharp knife. Brush with milk and bake in a preheated hot oven, 220°C (425°F), Gas Mark 7, for 25 to 30 minutes.

Serve with butter and preserves or honey.

Serves 12

NOTE: If buttermilk is unobtainable, use half fat milk and half natural low-fat yogurt instead.

MILK LOAF

500 g (1 lb) plain flour
1 teaspoon salt
40 g (1½ oz) butter
300 ml (½ pint) milk
15 g (½ oz) fresh yeast
1 teaspoon caster sugar
1 egg
1 egg yolk, to glaze

Have all the ingredients at room temperature except the milk, which should be heated without boiling.

Sift the flour with the salt into a warmed mixing bowl. Leave to stand in a warm place. Put the butter in the milk and leave it to melt. Combine the yeast with the sugar. Beat the egg in a bowl and stir in the milk mixture and the yeast and sugar. Make a well in the centre of the flour and pour this mixture into it.

Stir briefly with a wooden spoon then knead by hand for 5 minutes. Turn the lump of dough over and push a hole in the middle with your finger. Cover the bowl with a clean tea towel and place in a warm, draught-free place for 1 hour to prove and double in size. Knead again for 2-3 minutes.

Divide the dough into 3 equal parts. On a lightly floured surface roll each piece into a long roll. Plait the strips to make a single loaf. Place on a baking sheet and brush lightly all over with beaten egg.

Place in a preheated oven at 180°C/350°F/Gas Mark 4 for 30 minutes. Turn on to a wire rack to cool.

Makes one 1 kg (2 lb) loaf.

LEFT: *Soda Bread*

RIGHT: *Herb Bread*

SESAME BAPS

500 g (1 lb) plain strong white flour
1 teaspoon salt
25 g (1 oz) butter
15 g (½ oz) dried yeast
1 teaspoon caster sugar
150 ml (¼ pint) milk
150 ml (¼ pint) water
15 g (½ oz) sesame seeds

Put the flour, salt and butter in a food processor and process for 10 seconds.

Mix the yeast and sugar together in a small bowl. Warm the milk and water, pour over the yeast and leave for 10 minutes. Pour down the feed tube and process for 1 minute.

Transfer to a bowl, cover loosely with clingfilm and leave in a warm place for about 2 hours, until doubled in size.

Return to the processor and process for 1 minute. Divide into 12 pieces and knead lightly. Roll out slightly to flatten, place on baking sheets and leave to rise in a warm place for 20 minutes.

Brush with water or milk and sprinkle with sesame seeds. Bake in a preheated hot oven, 220°C (425°F), Gas Mark 7, for 15 minutes, until risen and golden. Cool on a wire rack.

Makes 12

BREAD TOPPINGS

There is very little to beat a good plain farmhouse or wholesome wholemeal loaf but sometimes a little more fancy is required. This can be easily achieved if you top your basic bread mixture with a variety of seeds and grains. Consider poppy seeds, bulgar wheat, buckwheat, grated cheese, toasted sesame seeds, chopped nuts, caraway seeds or dried herbs prior to cooking – they all give an interesting crust to the bread.

HERB BREAD

450 ml (¾ pint) warm milk
1 tablespoon dried yeast
1 teaspoon black treacle
1 tablespoon dried mixed herbs
375 g (12 oz) plain flour
2 teaspoons salt
375 g (12 oz) wholemeal flour
25 g (1 oz) butter

Mix together the milk, yeast, treacle and herbs; set aside for 10 minutes.

Sift the plain flour and salt into a bowl, then stir in the wholemeal flour. Rub in the butter. Add the milk mixture; mix to a firm dough.

Turn onto a floured surface and knead for 5 minutes until smooth and elastic. Place in a clean bowl, cover with a damp tea-towel and leave to rise in a warm place for 1 hour or until doubled in size.

Turn onto a floured surface and knead again for a few minutes. Cut in half and either place in two 500 g (1 lb) greased loaf tins, or shape into rounds and put on greased baking sheets. Leave to rise in a warm place for 30 minutes.

Bake in a preheated hot oven, 230°C (450°F), Gas Mark 8, for 30 minutes or until the loaves sound hollow when tapped. Cool on a wire rack.

Serves 20

INDEX

H

I

J

K

L

M

N

O

P

Q

R

S